# THE MODERN FORMULA 1 RACE CAR

## FROM DRAWING BOARD TO RACETRACK

# THE MODERN FORMULA 1 RACE CAR

## FROM DRAWING BOARD
## TO RACETRACK

Nigel Macknight

*Motorbooks International*
Publishers & Wholesalers ®

First published in 1993 by Motorbooks International Publishers and Wholesalers, P O Box 2, 729 Prospect Avenue, Osceola, WI 54020, USA

Library of Congress Cataloging-in-Publication Data
Macknight, Nigel
    The modern Formula 1 race car/Nigel Macknight
        p. cm. Includes index
    ISBN 0-87938-823-4
    1. Formula 1 automobiles – Design and construction. I. Title.
    II. Title: Modern Formula 1 race car.
    TL236.M317   1993
    629.228 – dc20   93-24762

Printed and bound in Hong Kong

**All photos by TC Allen/Photosphere, Huntingdon, England** – except where credited below.

Front cover (main image), *Autosport*; page 1, Steven Tee/LAT Photographic; pages 2/3, *Autosport*; page 7, *Autosport*; page 9, *Autosport*; page 10, *Autosport*; page 12, *Autosport*; page 31, *Autosport*; page 32, Lola BMS-Ferrari; page 33, Lola BMS-Ferrari; page 135, Yamaha/Jardine PR; page 189, *Autosport*; page 190, *Autosport*; page 191, *Autosport*.

**Page design:** Macknight International, Grantham, England

**Page makeup:** GA Graphics, Stamford, England

**Dedicated to the memory of Paul Breeton**

# Contents

# Acknowledgements

*The Modern Formula 1 Race Car* would not have been possible without the wholehearted cooperation of Lola Cars. For a period of six months, I was an almost daily visitor to the company's premises in Huntingdon, Cambridgeshire. I am indebted to Eric Broadley for granting me unrestricted access to view the activities that brought a new Grand Prix car into existence.

Colin Whittamore, who coordinated the construction of the Lola BMS-Ferrari T93/30, was my primary point of contact at Lola Cars. He accommodated persistent demands on his time without complaint, under the pressure of getting three cars ready for the first Grand Prix of 1993: a testimony to his kindness and professionalism.

I am grateful to Mike Blanchet and Brian Sims for the part they played in negotiating the terms under which this book was produced – Mike also read the draft manuscript and offered suggestions prior to publication – and indebted to everyone at Lola Cars and Lola Composites who answered technical questions and assisted when we took photos.

Finally, thanks to Tim Parker and Michael Dregni at Motorbooks International, and to Geoff Emery at GA Graphics.

# Introduction

This book offers an insight into the creation of a modern Formula 1 car. I did not attempt to produce the definitive treatise on Formula 1 race-car engineering, for that would be beyond my capabilities. Rather, my intention was to illuminate some of the darker corners of the subject for the benefit of motorsport enthusiasts wanting to learn more about what takes place 'behind the scenes.'

To approach the subject from a practical, as opposed to theoretical standpoint, I've traced the progress of one car – the Lola BMS-Ferrari T93/30 – from drawing board to racetrack. The design and construction techniques described and illustrated are, however, generic to Formula 1, and are therefore relevant to all contemporary Grand Prix racing cars.

The American author Leon Mandel, in *Speed with Style* – the autobiography of Grand Prix racing driver Peter Revson – said: "A race car is a lean and terrible thing. Delicate, highly bred, it is like a fine horse but with an immense strength no living creature can have."

This book dissects the beast, exposing the sinews and musculature for all to see.

Nigel Macknight
Lincolnshire,
England
May 1993

# CHAPTER
# 1

# Why Formula 1?

**The astronomical cost of competing at Formula 1 level means that, without a sound commercial approach, no team can hope to participate for long.**

Behind every Formula 1 car today, there's a business plan. The days when wealthy privateers could roam from race to race for the sheer pleasure of it have long since disappeared. The astronomical cost of competing at Formula 1 level means that, without a sound commercial approach, no team can hope to participate for long.

The commercial rationale behind each team varies. Ferrari goes racing primarily to uphold its reputation as the manufacturer of exotic street cars. That effort is underwritten by Ferrari's parent organization – the mighty Fiat empire – which, in turn, benefits by association. Another top team, Benetton, goes racing to promote the range of 'designer' clothing it markets through hundreds of stores across the world. Benetton's current involvement in Formula 1 is the product of a business plan that grew with time. The Italian clothing giant entered the arena as a sponsor of the Tyrrell team in the early-1980s, then bought a share of a different team (Toleman), and now *is* a team in its own right.

Williams and McLaren, the dominant forces in Formula 1 over recent years, have maintained their esteemed status because their expertise enables them to command massive sponsorship fees fulfilling the aspirations of others. Williams enabled Renault to achieve a goal it had been incapable of achieving on its own, by garnering the 1992 World Championship. Prior to that, McLaren did the same for another automotive colossus, Honda. Of course, both Renault and Honda had contributed to their respective successes by supplying engines of outstanding quality.

Lola's entry into Formula 1 in 1993 superseded several forays by the Huntingdon company into motorsport's premier league. Having supplied chassis to various Formula 1 teams in the distant past, Lola engaged in a liaison with the French Larrousse team for five consecutive seasons, 1987 to 1991. The relationship with Larrousse was such that Lola had insufficient control over the engineering aspects – a problem that was compounded in 1991, when Larrousse got into financial difficulties.

As of April 1993, Lola was still seeking legal recourse for monies owed for work undertaken for the Larrousse team during the course of 1991. Gerard Larrousse's company went into liquidation, so Lola was dealing with the liquidators through the French courts. Not an easy task.

Lola Cars' Joint Managing Director, Mike Blanchet, was typically forthright in explaining the background to Lola's latest Formula 1 effort. A Jerseyman who worked in a sales/managerial capacity for Rank-Zerox before joining Lola, Blanchet became the company's works driver in Formula Ford 1600 in 1976, and went on to compete in Formula Ford 2000, Sports 2000, and finally Formula 3 – driving factory-supported Lolas throughout. He also undertook development testing of all of the company's models, with the exception of the Can-Am and Indy models. Blanchet's blend of business experience and finesse behind the wheel appealed to Eric Broadley, who recruited him into Lola's management team. He stopped competitive driving in 1985, because Lola had grown to the extent that he felt he must concentrate 100 percent on the business.

Blanchet believes that the origins of the current Formula 1 project can be traced back to a year or

so after Lola embarked on its ill-starred partnership with the Larrousse team. "I think that our involvement with Larrousse proved a couple of things. One, that there was nothing for us to be afraid of from a technical standpoint in Formula 1 – although, clearly, starting from scratch again, it's going to be difficult in the early stages getting a feel for it. That aside, Formula 1 is really no different from any other category of racing. You have to accept that the level of effort and money is higher, but there's nothing frightening about the technology. I suppose, until you're involved, you do wonder about that.

"The other side of the coin was that it soon became apparent that the only way we could compete successfully in Formula 1 was by having far more control over the engineering. The arrangement we had with Larrousse, and the kind of personalities involved, really precluded that from happening.

"It became clear to us that we needed to be in Formula 1 in our own right."

The arrangement Lola's directors eventually came to ensured the degree of engineering control they needed. It was to be a long-term, wholly collaborative partnership with the Italian team BMS Scuderia Italia – the initials stand for Brixia (Latin for Brescia) Motor Sport. BMS Scuderia Italia had hitherto campaigned cars supplied by the Italian manufacturer Dallara Automobili, achieving creditable results. For their part, the directors of BMS Scuderia Italia saw the partnership with Lola as an opportunity – given sufficient time and effort – to become a front-running team.

Before outlining the reasons for reentering Formula 1, Mike Blanchet was quick to dispel any notion that Lola might kill the goose that lays the golden eggs: "Make no mistake, we still want production racing cars to be a major part of our business. Historically, we've always done very well at that, and there's no way that we're going to drift away from our roots. In fact, there are many advantages the Formula 1 program can bring to our core businesses.

"The reasons for reentering Formula 1 are mani-

*Ferrari goes racing primarily to uphold its reputation as the manufacturer of exotic street cars. That effort is underwritten by Ferrari's parent organization – the mighty Fiat empire – which, in turn, benefits by association.*

9

*McLaren and Williams, the dominant forces in Formula 1 over recent years, have maintained their esteemed status because their expertise enables them to command massive sponsorship fees fulfilling the aspirations of others. That includes Honda and Renault, both of which were unable to achieve the ultimate success single-handedly.*

fold. On the one hand, there's a line of thought that says: The company's products have been successful in every other category of motor racing it's been involved in, so why not Formula 1? You can also draw a parallel with the old justification for climbing Mount Everest. It's there! But there are some good, sound business reasons, too. You've got to be very wary of going into a project for any of the other reasons. At the end of the day, we *are* in business – and we have a responsibility to our employees, to their livelihoods.

"Our Formula 1 effort certainly isn't down to a personal ego thing on the part of the directors, because I think we've all been in racing long enough to take a fairly pragmatic view of it. Formula 1 doesn't have any starry-eyed appeal."

Blanchet's views as to why Lola should reenter Formula 1 were wholly supported by the company's founder, Chairman and Joint Managing Director, Eric Broadley. Between them, Broadley and Blanchet identified five reasons for reentering Formula 1. They

can be categorized as: doctrinal, financial, technological, promotional and social. These motives are examined in greater depth below.

**Doctrinal:** Eric Broadley emphasizes the need for growth for its own sake. "A commercial company, which we are, needs to expand. Not necessarily *every* year, but there does need to be a trend towards growth – growth over a period of time. Of course, you get wastage. Formulas are abolished from time to time, causing the market to temporarily shrink.

"Like any manufacturing entity, we're trying constantly to employ our full potential – to keep the workforce and the facilities fully occupied – because our standing costs remain the same whether we're working to full capacity or not."

Broadley's doctrinal commitment to growth has a lot to do with the way a company such as Lola is financed. To keep capitalizing – financing the acquisition of new, ever- more-expensive equipment to maintain its place at the forefront of international race car production – Lola has got to keep growing. It's analogous to a person running down a hill. He'll fall if he attempts to slow down, so he must constantly keep running that little bit faster.

Of course, there are dangers inherent in a policy of constant growth, and Broadley appreciates the fact. He cites the recent experience of Japanese industry, and maintains that the same dangers exist at a lower level. "In Japan's case, it's a question of over-production and the diminishing of foreign markets – the contraction of markets due to the worldwide recession. That's exactly what we have, but on a smaller scale. There *is* a danger. That's why we're looking to expand into Formula 1, and maybe other areas."

Broadley's reference to "other areas" may prove to include a street-legal supercar akin to Jaguar's XJ220, McLaren's F1 and Yamaha's OX99. Lola conducted a feasibility study into just such a concept several years ago, but shelved plans as the global recession worsened.

**Financial:** Mike Blanchet identifies this as probably the most important single factor. "With the economic decline that the world has got into, and therefore the contraction of the motor racing industry, Formula 1's actually the safest area to be in. Because it's the top of the tree, because it's the one that makes the whole thing work, it's the category all the powers-that-be are going to protect to the end. You've got to face the fact that, if there's a smaller sponsorship pie, what happens is that Formula 1 gets a bigger chunk of it – and that means there's less for everything else."

In early-December 1992 – many months after the directors of Lola Cars opted to embark on the new project – an edict issued from the Paris headquarters of motorsport's governing body, the Federation Internationale du Sport Automobile (FISA), highlighted the concerns that had driven the company towards Formula 1. FISA announced that Formula 3000, one of Lola's core markets, was going to be cancelled in 1994 due to rising costs, and replaced by a different formula. Hard on the heels of this news came FISA's decision to abolish the Group C sports-prototype formula.

Blanchet: "Categories such as Formula 3000 are very vulnerable to the shifting sands of politics at FISA. Those sorts of decisions, which seem to be able to be made fairly arbitrarily by the governing bodies, can have a very significant effect on a commercial organization such as ours. Therefore, we need to some extent to be protected against that. Being involved in Formula 1 is an obvious way."

To some extent, this part of the story has a happy ending. A few months later, Formula 3000 gained a reprieve, when parties with a commercial interest in its future – including Lola Cars – campaigned successfully to have a package of cost-cutting measures introduced, so that a revised Formula 3000 could continue for 1994 and beyond. Furthermore, it seemed likely that the title traditionally accorded to international single-seater motor racing's second most prestigious formula – Formula 2 – would be resurrected as part of the new image.

**Technological:** During the four years prior to the end of the 1992 season, Formula 1 underwent a period of unprecedented technological development. With the emergence of semi-automatic gearboxes, active and reactive suspension systems, and traction control – and with anti-lock braking systems (ABS) appearing on the horizon – the directors of Lola Cars came to the conclusion that the company must become a part of Formula 1 to assure its long-term survival. In short: if they weren't at the cutting edge, there was a danger of being left behind by those who were.

Mike Blanchet: "Okay, one could say we haven't been involved in it – until recent times – with any continuity, and it hasn't harmed our success, but I think you've got to react to what is a changing world. Every category is getting more competitive, and we have to take note of that.

"Being in Formula 1 does enable you to keep abreast of the latest technologies, even though a lot of those are banned from production racing cars. For instance, active suspension is banned from IndyCar racing. You still, nonetheless, learn from an involvement in that, and there might be an indirect benefit that you pick up. Despite the fact that Larrousse didn't undertake any development – because they never had the budget to do it – we could see that we had definitely gained something."

Moves to limit the use of some, if not all, of the technologies listed above began in the winter of 1992, and were gaining momentum as this book closed for press. While these might negate *some* of Lola's original reasons for reentering Formula 1, there would still be ample benefit, as Mike Blanchet explained: "It tends to be an overall cultural view. For instance, some of the technology necessary to make a Formula 1 car that's down on the weight limit – which our cars for Larrousse always were – we've been able to spin off into our production race cars in a way that we never thought would have been possible.

"Another example: three or four years ago, I don't think we would have anticipated being able to pro-

Formula 1 is a high-profile sport, offering Lola an opportunity to become known beyond the motor racing realm. If, at some future date, the company expands into other areas, the promotional benefits of a Formula 1 presence will pay dividends. One potential area of expansion is the development of a street-legal supercar akin to Jaguar's XJ220, McLaren's F1 (pictured here) and Yamaha's OX99.

ductionize the composite components that we use in the cars to the degree that we do, and yet retain the attention to detail in terms of weight-reduction and quality. The same applies to items such as uprights, which we fabricate. It's all very well doing it for Formula 1, where you're maybe making twenty or thirty sets maximum a year, as opposed to when you're making two or three hundred as part of a proper production run, but we have found through our Formula 1 involvement that it is feasible to do that, and to do it with some cost-effectiveness.

"Our involvement in Formula 1 led the way for us. We gained familiarity. We found that some things weren't as difficult as they appeared on the surface. It also pointed out areas that are very critical that *have* to be attended to, and I guess we learned that more quickly by being involved in Formula 1."

The technological spinoff works both ways – which is something Lola, uniquely among the teams involved in Formula 1, can benefit from. Mike Blanchet:

"There's an awful lot to be gained from being involved with other categories of motor racing, away from Formula 1. Lateral thinking is promoted, very definitely. Most people in Formula 1, indeed most people who concentrate on one area of racing only, tend to be very blinkered. They only look at what other people within their own sphere are doing. I think that's very dangerous.

"We look at racing globally. We're the only company actually able to do that, which I think gives us a significant advantage.

"Being involved in the large-scale production of racing cars also gives you a very sensible baseline from which to work. Because you can only spend what you earn – as opposed to the amount of sponsorship you can raise, which is normally the case in Formula 1 – it concentrates the mind wonderfully. Instead of diluting your effort by trying to do too many things, you tend to concentrate on two or three areas that you are pretty convinced are going to show a return. You concentrate all your resources on those

areas, and you do get a positive result out of it."

**Promotional:** Lola's directors feel there are considerable promotional benefits to having a presence in Formula 1. Formula 1 is a high-profile sport, with television coverage exceeded only by the Olympic Games and the soccer World Cup – held just once every four years, as opposed to sixteen times a year. Formula 1 offered Lola an opportunity to become known beyond the motor racing realm, as Mike Blanchet explained: "If we're looking, at some future date, to expand into other areas, it can only help if Lola is known within company boardrooms, and within the financial institutions, and among the ranks of the general public.

"If you're not involved in Formula 1, you may be doing a very good job, but you only get acknowledgment within a fairly limited sphere."

**Social:** Blanchet believes that the impact of the Formula 1 program on Lola's workforce should not be underestimated. "We haven't really had a situation whereby Lola itself could run a proper works race team, because we don't want to be competing against our customers – be it in IndyCar racing, or Formula 3000, or whatever. The Formula 1 project gives us the opportunity to go racing as a company, without any conflict of interests with our customers. That's good for the motivation and morale of our workforce. They're a very a competitive bunch. It's *their* team, and they can get behind it.

"I think our workforce is second to none. We've got some bloody good, committed people in the company – highly motivated engineers, for instance – and it's almost the case that we need to be able

to offer them the ultimate in order to retain their enthusiasm, and maybe to retain them over the longer term.

"It also helps from the point of view of recruiting young engineers. You tend to get the cream. Because you've got an involvement in Formula 1, they at least can see that they have the opportunity to get into Formula 1 – and I suppose, to some extent, any young engineer getting into motor racing *does* have a desire to get into Formula 1, because it's perceived as the pinnacle."

While extolling the virtues, Blanchet was equally aware of the potential pitfalls. The danger, for example, of Lola's workforce – or a sizeable proportion of it – becoming too focused on Formula 1, less enthusiastic about the company's other programs. Blanchet: "That is a danger, for sure. We've also got to be very careful we don't make the mistake that I think March made, for instance, when they went into Formula 1. They sucked all the good people out of the production side of their operation and assigned them to the Formula 1 program, leaving a vacuum behind.

"I don't see that happening here, mainly because we made it a matter of policy right from Day One that the Formula 1 project is treated the same as we treat all our projects. It is no different. It's a *company* project: we haven't got a separate organization just looking after the Formula 1 effort.

"Also, we have a system within the company, whereby projects don't rely too heavily on any one person. If people get moved around from one project to another, we see that as being extremely beneficial. We will want to maintain that."

*Building three Lola BMS-Ferrari T93/30s helped the drive to exploit the excellent facilities at Huntingdon. Says Eric Broadley: "Like any manufacturing entity, we're trying constantly to employ our full potential – to keep the workforce and the facilities fully occupied – because our standing costs remain the same whether we're working to full capacity or not."*

13

# CHAPTER 2
# The search for sponsorship

**The start of the search**

Raising sponsorship is as important to a Formula 1 team as any of the engineering aspects. If a team is inadequately financed, it will simply stagnate. Sponsorship-hunting is an industry in its own right these days – which is not surprising when one considers the sums of money involved. When the directors of Lola Cars made their decision to field a works Formula 1 team, they calculated they'd require sponsorship totalling approximately $20 million (£12 million) for the first season's racing. This is an average Formula 1 budget. Teams at the back of the grid struggle along with considerably less, while some at the front spend several times that amount. Former racing driver Brian Sims is responsible for coordinating Lola's sponsorship-raising activities. Sims raced in Formula Ford 1600 in Britain from 1974-1979. He moved to South Africa in 1980, becoming manager of the Kyalami circuit and commentating on races for South African television and radio stations. He raced showroom stock (Group N) cars and Group C sports-prototypes professionally from 1983-1987, then retired from competitive driving to open a racing drivers' school at Kyalami.

Sims first became involved with Lola at the beginning of 1991, following an approach to Joint Managing Director Mike Blanchet, whom he'd first met in the mid-1970s. Blanchet recalls Sims as a driver who always seemed to have the benefit of major sponsorship. For the first six months, Lola retained Sims on a consultative basis. His brief was to initiate the sponsor-finding process for a comprehensive Formula 1 program.

Enter the global recession, which put a very different perspective on things. Brian Sims: "We soon realized that it was going to be a *lot* tougher than we'd anticipated. I think that's true of all teams, not just Lola. I started by contacting a lot of companies on a one-to-one basis. With my previous involvements in motorsport, I had a fairly good contact base around the world."

During this period, Sims travelled to America (twice), Japan, and – exploiting contacts he'd established whilst living there – South Africa. There, he approached the Sasol oil company, headquartered in Johannesburg. Sasol, which had sponsored Sims' racing drivers' school at Kyalami, *did* enter Formula 1 the following year – but not with Lola. Sims explained how such a thing could come about: "I had a very good relationship with Sasol, so I went down to see them. Unfortunately, the tax incentives in South Africa were due to change on the 1st of April 1991, and we didn't have a team to offer them in time to beat that deadline. In the end, the Jordan team – which *was* in a position to offer a Formula 1 program for the 1992 season – landed the Sasol deal. Otherwise, I think we could have got it."

Despite the oppressive economic climate, efforts to raise the necessary backing continued. On October 1, 1991, a new company – Lola Motor Racing Management – was formed to coordinate sponsorship activities, with Sims as its Marketing and PR Director. To enhance its effectiveness, the company appointed a North American representative in November 1991: Entertainment Properties of Bridgeport, Connecticut was retained on a twelve-month contract.

The selection of Entertainment Properties was a logical step, as this company had previously undertaken sponsor- hunting for Newman-Haas Racing – the team run by Lola Cars' North American agent, Carl Haas, who has a long history of fielding teams in major American championships, notably the IndyCar series. Within a matter of weeks, a prospective deal – one well capable of fulfilling Lola's Formula 1 ambitions – emerged. Brian Sims, working in conjunction with Barry Chappel of Entertainment Properties, approached the European headquarters of one of the major international oil companies: Texaco. They believe they came within a hair's breadth of landing a $16 million (£10 million) deal.

"Unfortunately", says Brian Sims, "the recession – the fall of the dollar at that time – hit very hard, which didn't help. Also, they felt they weren't ready to exploit the huge sums of money that were going to be spent, because their own infrastructure was not in place to go Formula 1 motor racing at that time. We looked, therefore, at putting together an embryo Formula 1 team – a Formula 3000 team that would effectively have been a Texaco-sponsored Lola factory team – with a view to taking that up into Formula 1 in 1994 or '95."

However, two events conspired to scotch this plan. One appeared, on the surface of it, to have no connection with motor racing – but in the world of high-profile public relations, it played its part nonetheless. It concerned Europe's tallest office complex, Canary Wharf in east London. Texaco was two-thirds of the way to transferring its European headquarters from London's fashionable Knightsbridge district (where the Harrod's department store is situated) to Canary Wharf when the company behind that ambitious enterprise went bankrupt. It was going to cost Texaco a lot of money to withdraw from Canary Wharf at such a late stage, and it would cost almost as much to move back to Knightsbridge.

Eventually, Texaco opted to complete the move to Canary Wharf, but this unhappy episode almost undoubtedly influenced the company's decision not to enter Formula 1. Sponsoring any Formula 1 team has its risks, and it's likely that Texaco did not care to chance what might be perceived as a second embarrassing situation so soon after the Canary Wharf debacle.

The other event that influenced Texaco's decision was the unexpected opportunity to exploit Nigel Mansell's name throughout Europe, when the Englishman – disenchanted with Formula 1 in general and the Williams team in particular – began to show a serious interest in joining the Newman-Haas IndyCar team, which Texaco already part- sponsored.

Brian Sims: "I have to say that, given the choice of spending in the region of $2.5 million on a Formula 3000 program, or – I don't know what it cost to get Mansell – but let's say putting that towards the cost of getting Nigel Mansell in the Newman-Haas team and using his name in Europe, there's no arguing that Texaco made the right decision. At least they were staying in the fold with Lola, so to speak, because we not only supply cars to Newman-Haas, but also have a very close relationship with them. Nevertheless, to me as the sponsorship coordinator for Lola Cars, it was a great disappointment not to have persuaded Texaco to undertake a Formula 1 program alongside its IndyCar involvement. We came very, very close.

"It's a strange job, looking for money. As an ex-racing driver, I have an ego. I'm motivated by the success of finding the money, rather than the commission that I would earn on it – although, obviously,

*Chasing the money. Former racing driver Brian Sims is responsible for coordinating Lola's sponsorship-raising activities.*

I like to have a nice lifestyle. When you've worked very hard, and put in a *tremendous* amount of effort, the day eventually comes when somebody says they aren't going to do it – and that hurts. It hurts very much indeed."

The Texaco deal was a lot of work to watch slip down the drain. Negotiations had commenced in December 1991, and the decision not to proceed came in July 1992.

It wasn't the only deal Sims pursued. There were several others that didn't get as close to bearing fruit. An approach was made to ITT, an international corporation headquartered in New York. ITT encompasses the Sheraton hotel group, an automotive division that markets Koni shock absorbers, and many other subdivisions. In the event, its automotive division – which had just decided to sponsor the Detroit Grand Prix, an IndyCar race – scotched an ITT group deal.

"We got a negative response to our proposal, purely because of the size of the budget required," says Sims.

In the same timeframe, another American-based international giant – Coca-Cola – came into the picture. Brian Sims takes up the story: "We were approached by a PR agency representing Coca-Cola. Of course, they're so big they don't just have one PR agency, but this company was one of those that represented them. We went as far as making presentations to Coca-Cola in Atlanta, but that was a very weird one because there was a tremendous amount of excitement that Coca-Cola were going to break away from their traditional policy of events-only sponsorship and suddenly come into Formula 1 with a team. With Lola being a very well-known name in the States, it seemed to make a lot of sense.

"The whole thing got very exciting and went to board level, and suddenly got thrown out totally on the basis of, 'Well, we never sponsor anything other than events.'

"We've never, ever, to this day, found out why there was all the excitement and suddenly the whole thing was canned. That is one of the frustrations when you're undertaking one of these sponsorship proposals: you very often never discover the *real* reason why your proposal was turned down.

"It's so easy, in difficult times economically, for a company to say, 'Ah, but we've been hit by the recession. We've had to cut our budget.' How do you argue with that? It's almost impossible – short of calling the guy a liar. Whereas, in the good times, it was more difficult for someone to cite that as the reason."

By now, Lola was running well behind the schedule set that spring. At such a late stage in the year, it was going to be difficult getting a new car designed, built and tested in time for the first Grand Prix of 1993 – then slated for 28 February. Fortunately, FISA slipped the date to 14 March some months later, but it was still going to be a close-run thing.

In July 1992, just a few days after the highly promising Texaco sponsorship deal had fallen through, events took a decisive turn. There came the first hint of an opportunity to go into partnership with an existing Formula 1 team – the BMS Scuderia Italia organization, based near Brescia in northern Italy.

Joining forces with an existing Formula 1 team would add substance and stability to a plan still very much in its infancy. Not least of many attractions was the Italian team's exclusive Ferrari engine deal, for sourcing a suitable engine package had become a knotty problem for Lola. BMS Scuderia Italia is the only team other than the Ferrari works team permitted to use the fabled V12 power unit. Sims: "I suppose it's fair to say that, while the Ferrari is certainly not as good at this moment as a Renault or a Honda, it is certainly *as good*, if not better, to be involved with Ferrari – with their development programs – than with one of the 'customer engine' suppliers."

BMS Scuderia Italia is but one small part of the huge Lucchini empire, headed by Dr. Giuseppe Lucchini. At its heart is Lucchini Steel – the principal supplier of non-ferrous metals to Fiat's factories in Italy, Poland and elsewhere. Through Fiat, Lucchini's products flow to the Ferrari factory at Modena in northern Italy. Thus, Dr. Lucchini has built up a close relationship with Fiat over the years, of which BMS Scuderia Italia's much-sought-after use of Ferrari racing engines is but one manifestion.

Engine research and development is particularly important in Formula 1, and Ferrari's efforts easily eclipse anything a 'customer engine' supplier can hope to mount. But Lola's directors – especially Brian Sims – were quick to perceive another benefit to the Ferrari connection. *Kudos!* The cachet of a famous name with which to lure sponsorship. "That name Ferrari! I don't care what anybody says – people can say it's not that good an engine – but in the boardroom of an international corporation, it makes a darn sight more sense than many of the other names one could mention."

An exploratory meeting took place at the British Grand Prix at Silverstone in mid-July. Sims met with Paolo Stanzani, Managing Director of BMS

Logos on this Lola BMS-Ferrari team transporter represent just part of the 'dowry' BMS Scuderia Italia was able to bring to its partnership with Lola Cars. Approximately two-thirds of the budget Lola's directors had calculated was necessary for a year of quality participation in Formula 1 was effectively assured by the Italian team's existing sponsors.

The Lola BMS-Ferrari T93/30's nose cone/front aerofoil ensemble bears allegiance to associate sponsors Framon lighting and Secol construction, joint associate/technical sponsor Magneti Marelli, and technical sponsor Goodyear (tires).

Scuderia Italia. "It really was a coincidence that, having lost that big sponsorship deal with Texaco, and with various other possibilities having fallen through, we suddenly found ourselves with the chance of doing a deal with BMS Scuderia Italia. They knew we were planning to enter Formula 1. For our part, we'd heard through the grapevine that they weren't too happy with Dallara, and that there was an opportunity – maybe – that they'd be interested in talking to us.

"We looked at what they had to offer and decided that, with the current economic climate, finding $20 million to start a brand new team was pretty unrealistic. I'm not saying it can't be done, because Sauber has just done it – but that's slightly different, because they've got Mercedes money

behind them."

Highlighting the difficulties of raising the necessary finance, several teams that planned to enter Formula 1 at the start of the 1993 season failed. Among them were the British outfit Pacific Racing, and the Spanish-based Bravo team, both of which had excelled in the lower formulas.

Brian Sims: "We came up with some pretty unique ideas and concepts for finding that money – for taking it further than just purely a sponsor/team relationship. One could take it into other areas, such as using the team as a means of introducing one sponsor to another, so they can do business together. At the end of the day, though, we weren't successful.

"I think, had we approached it three or four years

ago, we'd have been able to do it on our own."

After the initial meeting at Silverstone, a great deal of travelling took place between Huntingdon and Brescia, as Eric Broadley, Mike Blanchet and Brian Sims rushed back and forwards to Italy for further discussions. "I don't think I've ever been along the autostrada as fast as we did for some of those meetings", Sims recalled with a wide grin. "Incredible, looking back on it now."

The formal announcement of a new partnership between Lola Cars and BMS Scuderia Italia was made at the beginning of August 1992, at the Hungarian Grand Prix at Budapest – the race at which Nigel Mansell clinched the Drivers' World Championship. At a special press conference, Sims and Broadley flanked BMS Scuderia Italia's Paolo Stanzani, and the project was outlined.

Speaking several months later, Brian Sims' enthusiasm for the new partnership was palpable: "It's a very exciting deal. We're very happy. It gives us access to a team that is very professional. They have a very good finishing record, and that tells us that they prepare their cars properly. What they lack is the research and development to go from being a middle-of-the-grid team to being one of the front-running teams. We know we've got that.

"I guess the weak link, if any, here at Lola is that – while we're good at research, development, and building cars – we don't have the direct experience of running a Formula 1 team. In the circumstances, it made a lot of sense to, 'Add one and one together to get three.' That's a term I use with potential sponsors.

"My own personal feeling is that you'll see more of this happening, not less. The budgets are getting incredibly big today for one company to raise on its own. I think that to bring together two organizations is the best way to go – provided, for us, it's not another Larrousse situation: one where we're not just supplying chassis, but actually have an involvement in the research, development and ongoing progress of that team."

After encountering such difficulties with Larrousse, why plunge back into potentially turbulent waters with a new partner? On this particular issue, Mike Blanchet voiced his views: "We feel that it's a very good opportunity for us. Although our original intention was to set the thing up entirely on our own, the facts of life are that we would not be able to get into Formula 1 at the entry level we can by being involved with BMS Scuderia Italia.

"We're pretty impressed with the team. They run a tidy operation. Bear in mind that they've only been around for four years, yet they've actually achieved quite a lot to date. We're particularly impressed with the involvement of Dr. Lucchini himself, who's obviously a man of considerable stature and substance, in Italy particularly, and seems to us a very strong but honorable sort of guy with a good background and a good reputation. We feel that fits in very well with what we are as a company.

"We seem to share the same objectives: being realistic and not expecting to go out and win in '93, but having some fairly clear objectives year on year as to what we want to achieve.

"Obviously, the big question mark with anything like this is whether the personalities gel, and there obviously are some logistical difficulties in operating with the team in Italy and the design and engineering base in the UK. However, our feeling is that if the *will* is there, then those difficulties can be overcome. The important thing is that the will is there to succeed. We believe it is. Only time will tell if we're correct, but certainly we're going to be giving everything we can, and we think Dr. Lucchini will do the same.

"There obviously is a cultural difference between the Italian way of doing things and the British way of doing things, but I don't think that's anything that can't be overcome – and if you use it in the correct manner, in fact, I see a positive benefit, in that each has got something different to bring to the table, and that can make the overall effort that much better.

"The Italians *do* run very good teams. Even at Ferrari. Okay, they're always screwed by the politics, but the *team* does a bloody good job. If you look at the pitstops, who do the best pitstops? Ferrari do! Consistently. You look at racing generally – in Formula 3000, for example – the most successful teams at the moment seem to be Italian teams.

"Where the Italian teams appear to be lacking is in the pure design area, and in the political aspects. They let too much politics get involved. But I think with Lucchini we've got a strong asset, in that he's a very clear-thinking guy, and I don't think he's going to let the politics get in the way of achieving what we set out to do."

Joining forces with the ambitious Italian equipe wasn't the end of Brian Sims' quest for sponsorship. Even before the opportunity arose to enter into partnership with BMS Scuderia Italia, Lola Motor Racing Management had been expanding on its policy of engaging agents overseas to increase its ability to raise sponsorship. Brian Sims explained the rationale behind this development: "Travel is a big

*Highlighting the difficulties of raising the necessary finance, several teams that planned to enter Formula 1 at the start of the 1993 season failed.*

problem. The cost of finding sponsorship today is colossal. You can have a fruitless trip to Japan, say: one in which you spend thousands of pounds and have nothing to show at the end of it.

"The language barrier is another problem, of course. Also, when you're trying to sell Formula 1 sponsorship in Saudi Arabia, for example, or in Korea, you need a specialist approach these days, because the way they do business is very different.

"For all of those reasons, the network agency system works. Unless your name's Guy Edwards, one person just can't do it on his own."

Sims was referring to former Grand Prix racing driver Guy Edwards, the doyen of motorsport sponsorship-hunters, who – after spending two decades introducing new companies into motor racing – now works as the sponsorship coordinator for the Lotus Formula 1 team. Sims was quick to qualify his remark. "Even Guy Edwards has a basis on which to work: a whole field of contacts he can go to, which he set up in the good times. If he hadn't got that, I don't think he would be achieving much, either.

"He's negotiated deals such as the one with Castrol for Lotus in Formula 1. The groundwork for that was laid some years ago, when he brought Castrol in as sponsors of the works Jaguar sports-prototype team – so, really, it was a case of taking an existing sponsor into other areas.

"I have tremendous respect for Guy for what he does, but I think if he were to start afresh today, he would find it pretty tough."

In June 1992, Lola Motor Racing Management appointed API International as its principal sponsorship agent in the Far East and Europe. Interestingly, the company's British division, APA, is run by former Olympic athlete Alan Pascoe.

The following month, several days before the momentous meeting with BMS Scuderia Italia's Paolo Stanzani at Silverstone, Lola Motor Racing Management contracted with Thoburn and Associates to represent its sponsorship interests in the Middle East.

In November 1992, when the twelve-month agreement between Lola Motor Racing Management and Entertainment Properties expired, API USA was contracted to assume the North American sponsorship-finding franchise.

Finally, in December, Sims arranged a similar deal with Motor Racing Enterprises – the company that possesses the rights to run all races on the Kyalami circuit – whereby they headed Lola's sponsorship drive in South Africa.

Having thus assembled a global network of spon-

sor-finding agencies, Sims was bullish about future prospects: "I've got a very strong feeling that we're going to get a lot of money out of the Middle East. It's an untapped area at the moment – a *hell* of a difficult one to get into. Williams did in it the early-1980s with a consortium of Saudi companies, but nobody since then has really achieved anything.

"Our API International people have just come back from a big tour of the Far East, and they'll be going back again. There's a *lot* of interest, believe me.

"My job has changed from being the person who goes out to find the sponsorship, to being the person who coordinates the search for sponsorship and gets involved in the later stages of the sponsorship bid. Instead of doing all the legwork, which for one person today is almost impossible, I work hand-in-glove with the members of our international network.

"In the last twelve months we've had a tremendous amount of media coverage, much of which has focused on our IndyCar involvement. The IndyCar connection is good, because a weak link in the sponsorship chain in Formula 1 today is America. Time and time again, I've approached companies and they've said, 'Look, Formula 1 in America – which is one of our primary markets – is virtually non-existent, and there's very little TV coverage.'

"A company goes into motor racing sponsorship, whether it's Formula 1 or whatever, to achieve business objectives. Williams, McLaren or Benetton can only offer Formula 1, and therefore, whatever the company wants to achieve has to be achieved through Formula 1. Here at Lola, we're able to offer a much wider package to companies. When it comes to finding money – particularly in today's market – I believe you have to look for something you can offer that nobody else can.

"Lola has the advantage of being able to offer in-depth penetration into the North American market, by creating a direct link between the Formula 1 program and Lola's big name in America. We can also offer that in Japan, through our Formula 3000 connections there.

"We're an internationally recognized company, and we have to use that to our best advantage. We can offer a comprehensive motor racing package, of which maybe 80 percent is the Formula 1 program, and the rest is an associate-sponsor involvement with any one of a number of Lola customers in, say, the American IndyCar series. Our IndyCars account for over two-thirds of the grid, so we could arrange a reciprocal deal with an American team with comparative ease."

*Transport company Setrans was one of several new associate sponsors introduced to the Lola BMS-Ferrari team by the Italian side of the partnership.*

An unusual product to see advertised on a race car. On the leading edges of the sidepod inlets are the logos of associate sponsor Almar – maker of door handles!

## A deal with a dowry

From the sponsorship standpoint, the newly inaugurated arrangement with BMS Scuderia Italia changed the ballpark totally. Brian Sims explained: "Whereas, before, I was selling a concept – and that's always difficult – now we can take potential sponsors to a race and show them the team and the Ferrari engines. Also, the driver lineup is known.

"The times are tough. It's not an easy job at any time, but it has certainly made the job easier. Before BMS Scuderia Italia came into the picture, we had to find a core sponsor willing to put in a minimum of $8-10 million – because unless you've got the core there, you can't sell any of the smaller sponsorship deals in case they're going to conflict with the potentially major one. With the new arrangement, there's already a sizeable proportion of the budget in place, because BMS Scuderia Italia has money from its existing pool of sponsors."

In fact, approximately two-thirds of the budget Lola's directors had calculated was necessary for a year of quality participation in Formula 1 was effectively in place the moment the contract with BMS Scuderia Italia was signed, because most of the Italian team's existing sponsors undertook to continue their backing of the team.

BMS Scuderia Italia's primary sponsor was Philip Morris (Italy), which had hitherto promoted its Marlboro cigarette brand. One level below that, but nevertheless injecting considerable sums of money, were the Italian oil company Agip, and Lucchini Steel. The latter, together with several other members of the Lucchini group that maintain a less prominent involvement with the team, do so because they recognize the benefits of exploiting Formula 1 for marketing purposes – and they pay for the privilege.

Only one major sponsor of BMS Scuderia Italia's 1992 effort decided not continue into 1993: the Italian finance company Fin-Eco.

Over time, many of the associate sponsors also elected to stay with the team, although the logos of some of them did not appear on the car at the time of its unveiling in Milan in early-March, and other logos were not scheduled to appear on the cars until the European segment of the 1993 World Championship started at Donington Park in April. The confirmed associate sponsors were lighting manufacturer Framon, automotive electronics specialists Magneti Marelli, the Secol construction company, door handle makers Almar, and the company that organizes the 1,000km Mille Miglia veteran car race.

In addition, several new associate sponsors joined the fold: Fastar optical accessories, Replay clothing, Osama writing instruments, and the Setrans transport company. The latter was due to be replaced later in the season by the Lusfina finance house - another company that sponsored BMS Scuderia Italia in 1992.

One prominent associate sponsor that supported BMS Scuderia Italia in 1992, the Camozzi engineering company, defected to McLaren for 1993, while at the time of writing, wine exporters Berlucchi had yet to renew their contract, and automotive technologists Spal were waiting to see how the new car performed in its first few races. Giochi, the domestic Italian importer of a wide range of Japanese-made computer games, had promoted two products – Megadrive and Gamegear – on the BMS Scuderia Italia cars in 1992, but looked unlikely to renew its contract for 1993.

A variety of companies agreed to support the team as technical sponsors. In addition to Agip (fuel and lubricants) and Magneti Marelli (electronics), the following companies agreed to supply products and/or services for the 1993 season: Goodyear (tires); Brembo (brake units); Carbone Industrie (brake discs); Due Emme Mille Miglia, a part of the Lucchini empire (wheel rims); Koni (dampers); Sparco (drivers' racewear); Momo (steering wheels); and USAG (tools).

Broad brush, the agreed demarkation of sponsorship monies between BMS Scuderia Italia and Lola Cars was as follows.

All monies accruing from existing sponsors was to go directly to BMS Scuderia Italia, together with monies accruing from new sponsors introduced by the Italian side of partnership. That was set aside to pay for the basic expenses involved in running a team – employing staff, travelling, and so forth.

Monies that Lola Motor Racing Management raised through its own efforts, and the efforts of its international network of sponsor-finding agents, were to go directly to Lola Cars. That would reimburse the cost of the three cars built for the partnership's initial entry into Formula 1, and the associated setting-up costs.

In both cases, there was an agreed ceiling to the sums raised. Monies over and above the agreed level were to go into a joint fund, primarily to finance an ongoing Formula 1 research and development program conducted at Huntingdon.

Brian Sims: "The difference between, say, a Williams setup and a Lotus setup at the moment is not the money that's spent at the racetrack, it's the money that's spent away from the racetrack – the funding for research and development. Here at Lola, we have

*Monies over and above the agreed level were to go into a joint fund, primarily to finance an ongoing Formula 1 research and development program .*

23

the resources to undertake a level of development a lot of the Formula 1 teams wouldn't be capable of. To pay for that, we need sponsorship money."

When the Lola BMS-Ferrari team came into being, Sims and his team had to change their entire strategy for negotiating sponsorship. Instead of having a blank sheet of paper and trying to raise massive sums of money, now they had to sell into the existing situation. One of the benefits was that they could concentrate on various associate sponsorship deals, without having to worry about finding a primary sponsor.

Sims had as his aim helping Lola BMS-Ferrari to contest the 1993 season with a fairly typical Formula 1 budget – somewhere in the region of $16-20 million (£10-12) million. He also planned to spend that year putting together a major, three-year sponsorship package, starting with the 1994 season, that would enable the team to grow from that point on. The target was a minimum annual budget of $25-27 million (£15-16 million).

With approximately $10-15 million (£6-9 million) already accounted for – albeit assigned directly to the Italian side of the partnership – Sims felt it was realistic to seek a minimum budget of $3.5 million (£2 million) for Lola's research and development effort before the start of the new team's inaugural season. If he and his agents could raise a certain amount more – say, $5-6.5 million (£3-4 million) – so much the better.

Sims, speaking in December 1992: "Our agency network is working very hard not to simply to pick up the odd £100,000 here and there. We're looking for *significant* sponsorship. These, ideally, will be multi-year contracts: two-year deals, with an option to go on for a third year. I don't believe that a sponsor gets anything out of it coming in for just one year. With multi-year deals, safe in the knowledge that the money's in place, we can embark on a research and development program that takes us from being on a platform in the middle of the grid to being a front-running team competing with the Benettons and the Williamses. *That* is our goal.

"Obviously, we have a reputation to protect. We can't enter Formula 1 in survival mode. We have to go in on the basis that from Day One, we're going to be fairly competitive."

Leaving aside the spaces reserved for BMS Scuderia Italia's original group of sponsors, Lola Motor Racing Management had about another $13 million (£8 million) worth of space available on the car. Only needing a minimum of $3.5 million (£2 million), the potential was there to earn a lot more than was strict-

ly necessary. Sims: "There's never going to be a ceiling to our sponsorship requirements for research and development. We will use every penny we can get."

"We're obviously working very hard on lots of potential sponsors at the moment, but we're very keen to find the right type of sponsor – the type that's going to enable us to do a proper program. We don't want the car covered in thousands of stickers that we've got to keep renegotiating all the time. What we want is a good sponsor who's going to stay with us and grow with us – as you've got Marlboro with McLaren, and Camel with Williams.

"We also want the right image. We don't want the name of a Columbian drug baron, for example, on the car."

Among the prominent corporations approached by Lola after the partnership with BMS Scuderia Italia began was Anheuser-Busch, the American-based owner of Budweiser beer. Sims says that, although they appreciate the benefits of Formula 1, the nature of Anheuser-Busch's own international licensing and franchising arrangements doesn't allow it to promote in many of the countries it would want to in order to gain the full benefit of a Formula 1-level spend. "The overall holding company in the States could spend, say, $8 million, but they told us they would never be able to recoup that in revenue to themselves."

Another disappointment was in store right on the eve of the 1993 season getting under way. It followed Lola's approach to the Japan-based makers of the phenomenally popular Sega computer games. Sims: "At a pretty senior level, Sega told us that they would not be interested, because the name of a cigarette company was on the car and they aim at the young person market, so they would not want that connection. They *assured* us that this was the reason. We went back to Philip Morris with a proposal that maybe we could do something that would not have such a visible presence of a cigarette company on the car – maybe just on the drivers. The Sega people ruminated on this and eventually decided that they weren't yet ready for an involvement Formula 1. Then, within the space of a month and a half, they signed with the Williams team, which has Camel's logos plastered all over its cars.

"That sort of thing is very frustrating! You can't argue with the fact that Williams could offer Sega guaranteed wins during the season, but they should have given that as the reason and not cited the cigarette connection. It would be nice if people were a bit more up-front."

Brian Sims elaborated on some of the difficulties involved in sourcing and signing major sponsorship deals for Formula 1 in the financially challenging 1990s. "I've been in the business since '74, so I've seen the ups and downs. What has happened in the sponsorship market is that the decision time, from the presentation of a proposal to actually getting a signature on a check, has stretched enormously.

"It's a buyer's market out there today, and companies are being approached left, right and center by people. Budgets are being cut back, invariably, and they know they don't have to rush into a decision. They know that if they put aside $2 million to go into Formula 1, that by March 14 – at the first race – if they go out to Kyalami and say 'We've got $2 million available, who wants it?' there's going to be at least one team ready and able to accept it.

"Furthermore, for the same amount of dollars, some teams are able to offer a prospective sponsor more publicity than the others, simply because they're further up the grid.

"Consequently, it's very difficult to put pressure on today to get that early signature."

Another difficultly Sims encountered was the reluctance of British companies to involve themselves in Formula 1 sponsorship. Although Britain is regarded as the 'home' of Formula 1, inasmuch as the vast majority of Grand Prix teams are based there, British industry fails to play a correspondingly prominent role when it comes to employing the sport for

*On the rear aerofoil endplates are the logos of Italian oil company Agip and the company that organizes the 1,000km Mille Miglia veteran car race.*

*In the absence of a major sponsor to purchase the spaces on the sidepod flanks, the Italian side of the partnership assigned some of it to the Agip oil company, and arranged for Lucchini Steel – part of the group that owns BMS Scuderia Italia – to occupy the remainder. Also in evidence are the logos of three of the team's technical sponsors: Brembo (brake units); USAG (tools); and Due Emme Mille Miglia, a part of the Lucchini empire (wheel rims).*

promotional purposes.

On Lola's behalf, Sims approached dozens of major British companies, only to encounter a wall of indifference. Sims: "We've been a little bit disappointed – as I guess everybody is – with the response of British industry to the sort of opportunities we've been offering. We approached some of the big corporations – British Gas, British Steel, the electricity generators – those sorts of people. I found the reticence to even *discuss* a proposal very difficult to comprehend. The telephonist or the secretary answering the phone effectively decides whether a major company's even interested in talking about Formula 1 sponsorship!

"The nice thing about American corporations is that you can get straight to the top so easily. You can phone a company, and the president or vice president will talk to you. You get *one chance* to talk to him, and if he's not interested in what you have

to offer – goodbye – but at least you can put your case.

"British companies seem to build this incredible wall between the decision-makers and those outside. It's seems that 99 percent of British industry is in meetings and can never be disturbed. It's rather like wanting to buy a motor car and you phone a garage and say, 'I want to come and buy a car,' and they say, 'Sorry, everyone's in a sales meeting.'

"If some of the top people in British industry made themselves a little more readily available, then it would improve matters for everybody. It's a great shame, because I do believe that British industry can benefit from Formula 1, but it doesn't even want to look at the opportunities in many cases.

"We made several approaches to Amstrad over the course of the last twelve months, and I must say that, despite every single attempt that we made to talk

with Alan Sugar, we never even got the courtesy of a reply to faxes, phone calls, anything. That is particularly frustrating: that there are British companies moaning like mad about a recession – of course, Amstrad's been particularly badly effected – not even prepared to listen to approaches, not from some little Tom, Dick or Harry, but a company that is incredibly successful in exports, a major British success story, that can't even get to see the chairman of another British company.

"I find that very, very sad – and maybe indicative of why we've got the problems."

Certain aspects of the 1992 Formula 1 season tarnished the image of the sport somewhat, and that certainly dealt a blow to its promotability for 1993. The season was notable for the acrimonious and highly publicized disputes between the three leading drivers – Frenchman Alain Prost, Englishman Nigel Mansell and Brazilian Ayrton Senna – and for the bitter comments Mansell directed at the team for whom he'd won that year's highest honors, Williams.

In addition, the nature of racetracks, and the stratification of teams according to the technological levels they had attained – the latter most graphically characterized by the overwhelming dominance of the Williams team – resulted in many races being little more than high-speed processions.

Several months after discussing the difficulties of raising sponsorship for a Formula 1 program, Brian Sims found himself pondering the fact that Lola Motor Racing Management had been unable to sign any sponsors by the time the 1993 season got under way at Kyalami, South Africa, on March 14.

Nevertheless, the two Lola BMS-Ferrari T93/30s appeared on the grid at Kyalami in a striking color scheme which bore no resemblence to that carried by BMS Scuderia Italia's Dallaras in 1992. Philip Morris (Italy), which had exhibited Marlboro markings on the cars throughout 1992, decided that for 1993 it would promote its Chesterfield brand instead. The distinctive logo had not been seen in Formula 1 since the late-1970s, when a succession of different cars bearing allegiance to the Chesterfield brand were fielded for the American driver Brett Lunger.

Brian Sims felt that the switch to Chesterfield could only be beneficial to Lola BMS-Ferrari, as it would establish a separate identity for the team, clearly distinguishing it from the two other teams with substantial Philip Morris backing – McLaren and Ferrari – which both bear allegiance to the Marlboro brand.

As for the dearth of Lola-found sponsors, Sims was disappointed but philosophical. "As we got steadily closer to the start of the season, potential sponsors were in a position to say that they wished to see how the car and team performed in the first couple of races before making a commitment. I think we'll see some sponsors signing contracts in time for the European segment of the World Championship, starting in April."

*Logo of the Anglo-Italian partnership.*

## Selling space

Each and every space on a Formula 1 car has a perceived value. The two diagrams reproduced here – part of the actual portfolio that Lola Motor Racing Management and its agents handed to potential sponsors up to the end of 1992 – reveal how the Lola BMS-Ferrari team delineated the spaces on its cars.

Note that Lola was not in a position to market all of the spaces on the car. The white areas represented zones already allocated to sponsors contracted directly to the Italian side of the partnership: BMS Scuderia Italia. Of the zones assigned to Lola to sell, the highest fee was that charged for the spaces on the sidepod flanks. The lowest fees were associated with spaces low down on the engine cover, just above the sidepods.

In the event, the Italians proved capable of sell-

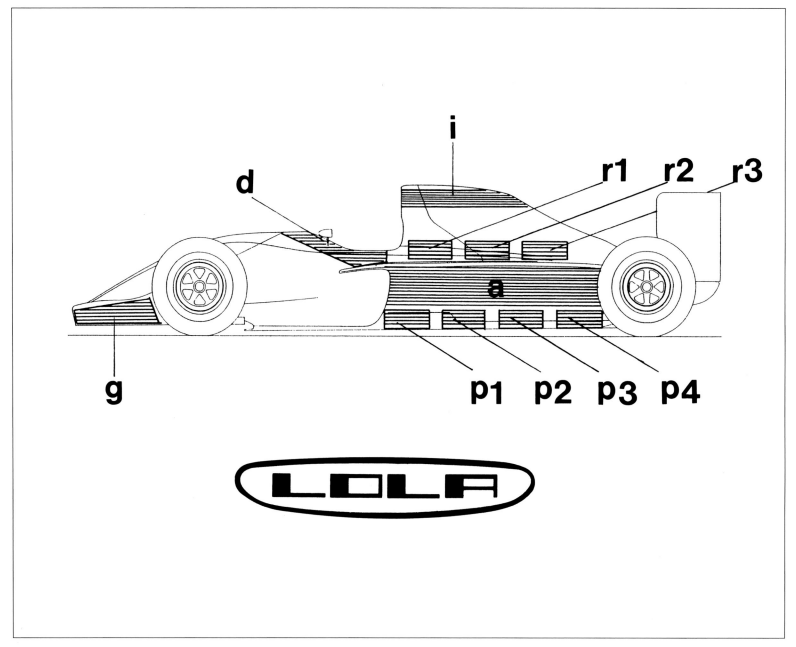

ing two sets of spaces their British counterparts couldn't. The spaces on the front aerofoil endplates were sold to the transport company Setrans, while in the absence of a major sponsor to purchase the spaces on the sidepod flanks, the Italians assigned some of it to the Agip oil company, and arranged for Lucchini Steel to occupy the remainder.

Within the zones delineated in the diagrams, there was provision for sponsors wishing to make a much smaller investment. Typically, such spaces are purchased by companies unable to justify – or, perhaps, to afford – a major involvement. They often supply a proportion of their sponsorship 'in kind.' For example, an international hotel group, when quoted a fee for one of these spaces, might agree to provide one-third of it in the form of accommodation to the team's personnel at race meetings around the world, and supply the remainder in cash.

*These two diagrams reveal how the Lola BMS-Ferrari team delineated the advertising spaces on its car for the 1993 Formula 1 season.*

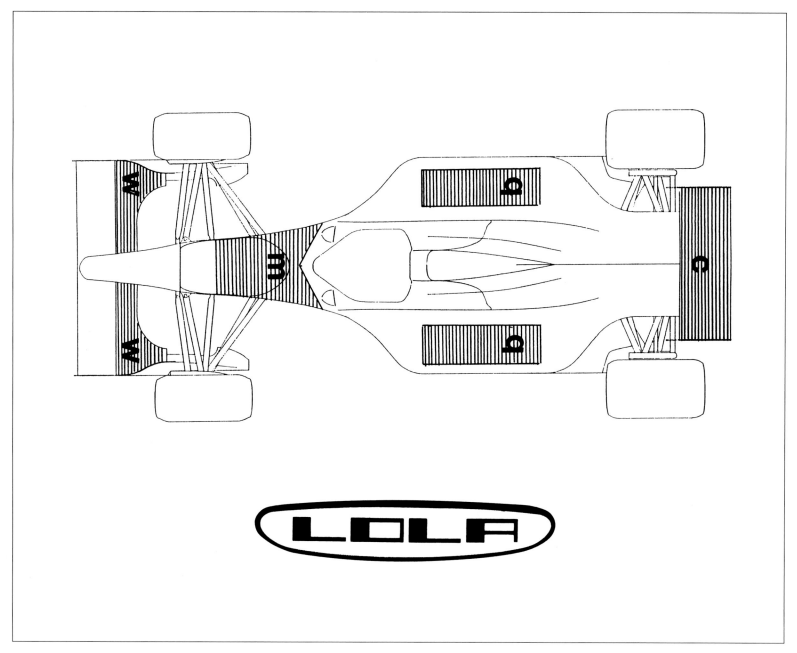

# CHAPTER

# 3

# Selecting drivers

**Often, teams take nationality into account when selecting their drivers. Ferrari's management, while not slaves to this credo, certainly allowed it to influence their decisions when Enzo Ferrari was in charge.**

Some Formula 1 teams hire drivers purely on merit. To them, the amount of sponsorship money a driver can bring with him is not a major factor. Teams such as McLaren, Williams, Benetton, Ligier, Lotus and Ferrari fall into this category. Other teams adopt the opposite policy, hiring their drivers solely on the basis of how much money they can bring with them. The financial status of these teams is such that this is the only way they can survive.

The March team typified this approach throughout the 1992 season, fielding no fewer than four different drivers during the course of the year – Karl Wendlinger of Austria, Paul Belmondo of France, Emanuele Naspetti of Italy, and Jan Lammers of Holland – in an effort to balance the books.

Often, teams take nationality into account when selecting their drivers. Ferrari's management, while not slaves to this credo, certainly allowed it to influence their decisions when Enzo Ferrari was in charge. Sometimes, a driver favored by the Italian public would be selected, come what may. Italians, of course, are renowned for their passionate enthusiasm for motor racing, and the pressure of public opinion in Italy – more often than not fuelled by overzealous press coverage – has, on occasion, caused Ferrari to make unwise choices as to its driver lineup.

Benetton, on the other hand, considers it a positive disadvantage to display strong nationalistic tendencies in its driver-selection process. Negotiations prior to the start of the 1991 Grand Prix season bore this out, when the vagaries of the driver-transfer market resulted in two extremely able Brazilians – double-World Champion Nelson Piquet, and his

protege Roberto Moreno – being available for the coming year. Common sense said they should sign both of them, thereby securing a strong lineup for the year ahead. Marketing considerations said otherwise: it might spoil the cosmopolitan image of the Benetton clothing chain to have two drivers of the same nationality in its racing team.

After much internal wrangling, Benetton's management finally relented to reason and signed both Piquet and Moreno – but it was a close-run thing!

The driver lineup of the Lola BMS-Ferrari team in its inaugural season, 1993, did not reflect any of these extremes. Nationality played a part (both drivers were Italian), but it didn't dominate the issue. Financial factors played a part (both drivers brought with them appreciable personal sponsorship), but money certainly wasn't the sole criterion. The agreement for 1993 was that a final decision as to the driver lineup would be made by the Italian side of the partnership, but that Lola's directors would be involved in the decision-making process.

Lola's directors had, as one might expect, already considered the question of a driver lineup, prior to striking the deal with BMS Scuderia Italia. Their favored driver was IndyCar star Michael Andretti, by now well-versed in driving Lola products to excellent effect. There was, however, a major complication in inviting Michael Andretti to join Lola's Formula 1 team: it would have meant coaxing him away from one of the company's most loyal customers, the Newman-Haas team, for whom Andretti had so nearly won the Indy 500 race that year.

For many teams in Formula 1, such niceties are not considered when it comes to signing drivers. The contractual wrangle between the Benetton and Jordan teams over Michael Schumacher in the middle of the 1991 season was a case in point. Lola's directors are not accustomed to such practices, and made no attempt to lure the rapid American away.

At a later date, Michael Andretti elected, of his own accord, to part company with Newman-Hass and contest the 1993 Formula 1 World Championship with the McLaren team.

Neither of BMS Scuderia Italia's drivers from the previous season feature in the current lineup. The way that came about exemplifies the machinations that take place in the majority of Formula 1 teams, where money, ability and nationality must all be taken into account.

BMS Scuderia Italia's drivers for the 1992 season were JJ Lehto of Finland, in his first season in Formula 1, and the more experienced Perluigi Martini of Italy. The Italian team was eager for Lehto – tipped as a future World Champion – to remain on-strength for 1993, and Lola's directors would certainly have supported this. However, the partnership between BMS Scuderia Italia and Lola was cemented at a late stage in the season, by which time Lehto – understandably disgruntled by the performance of his Dallara-built chassis – had been successfully courted by another organization gearing up for an assault on Formula 1: the Swiss-based, German-financed Sauber team.

With JJ Lehto out of the picture, the search began for a new team leader. Andrea de Cesaris, who had long-standing ties with the Italian arm of the Philip Morris group – proprietor of the Marlboro brand, and BMS Scuderia Italia's principal sponsor – became a candidate. Philip Morris (Italy) has a direct say in who drives for the team.

At around this time, the Ferrari factory exerted some subtle influence. As one might expect, Ferrari has a keen interest in the progress of BMS Scuderia Italia: the only team other than the works team to be granted a supply of its fabled V12 engines. Ferrari's management felt that, to help develop the new car, Michele Alboreto – with his twelve years of experience in Formula 1 driving for the Tyrrell, Ferrari, Lola-Larrousse (yes, Alboreto drove a Lola-built chassis in Formula 1 as long ago as 1989!) and Arrows/Footwork teams – would be ideal. His current contract with the British-based Footwork team, for whom he had performed admirably – finishing in the points four times and scoring six seventh-place finishes during the course of the 1992 season – was drawing to a close.

BMS Scuderia Italia and Lola felt likewise. Alboreto

*When Lola's directors first considered the question of a driver lineup, their preference for the number-one seat lay with IndyCar star Michael Andretti.*

– who took the runner-up spot in the Driver's World Championship for Ferrari in 1985, and had a total of five Grand Prix victories to his credit – would represent a known factor in an uncertain equation. He also had the benefit of a long-standing personal sponsorship arrangement with Philip Morris/Marlboro. Negotiations were therefore concluded with Alboreto.

For the record, another former Ferrari driver of Italian nationality – Ivan Capelli – was also considered for the number-one seat. So, too, was Roberto Moreno.

The search for a number-two driver also involved several players. BMS Scuderia Italia and Perluigi Martini having failed to agree terms, Lola's directors suggested Mark Blundell, with whom they'd worked closely in World Sports-Prototype racing. The gutsy Englishman had put a Nissan-badged Lola R90C (T90/10) on pole position for the Le Mans 24-Hour Race two years earlier. Blundell was no newcom-

*Following subtle influence on the part of the Ferrari management, Michele Alboreto – with his twelve years of experience in Formula 1, including five Grand Prix victories – was signed to lead the Lola BMS-Ferrari team. He represented a known factor in an uncertain equation.*

er to Formula 1: he undertook a full season with the Brabham team in 1991. Lola's directors felt that Blundell might even be a candidate for joint number-one status alongside Michele Alboreto for 1993.

There were complications with signing Mark Blundell, however, because the McLaren Formula 1 team – whom Blundell served as its contracted test driver – had an option to retain his services until early-December. In discussions with Lola's Brian Sims, Blundell did not attempt to hide the fact that he would re-sign for McLaren if they offered him a seat in the race team.

Another difficulty blighted Mark Blundell's candidature. There having been the usual lackluster response from British companies, Blundell had no personal sponsorship of any substance. For most Formula 1 teams these days, a dearth of personal sponsorship is enough to put a driver out of the running. Had Blundell been one of the many drivers who benefit from personal sponsorship from Philip Morris, a deal could have been possible.

Blundell went on to sign for the French team Ligier.

Damon Hill was another attractive proposition – mainly because, like Blundell, he had considerable Formula 1 testing experience: in this case, with the Williams team. He also had a limited amount of actual race experience in Formula 1, with Brabham. However, an absence of hard cash put the brakes on the deal once again. Despite possessing considerable talents and the promotional clout of being the son of legendary double-World Champion Graham Hill, Damon had no appreciable personal sponsorship behind him.

Subsequently, Damon Hill was signed by Williams to serve as its number-two driver to Alain Prost.

After all the discussions, a young hotshoe named Luca Badoer got the job. Being an Italian, Badoer was naturally of great interest to BMS Scuderia Italia. For their part, Lola's directors already knew more about Badoer than many of the more illustrious names being associated with the fledgling team at that time. He had come to their attention as the driver of a car that was often capable of beating Lolas in FIA International Formula 3000 Championship events – a Reynard entered by the Italian-based Crypton team (nevertheless, Badoer won that series).

Despite his achievements in Formula 3000, Luca Badoer's appointment was the subject of a little soul-searching at Lola. Soon after the 21-year-old was signed to the team, Brian Sims – who was regularly consulted during the driver- selection process – confirmed: "We had some reservations about Badoer.

He was very young, and had no prior experience in Formula 1. But then, who'd have said that Michael Schumacher could come straight into Formula 1 and do what he did? We talked to the Italians. He had sponsorship that he was able to bring to the team, as well – which swung the balance in his favor.

"We came to feel that the combination of a very experienced driver like Michele Alboreto, and a hungry young driver like Luca Badoer, obviously with a lot of talent, could be the ideal one for the '93 season."

*Young Italian hotshoe Luca Badoer got the job as Lola BMS- Ferrari's number-two driver, after winning the 1993 FIA International Formula 3000 Championship.*

# CHAPTER 4

# Defining the concept

**Theoretical ideals must invariably give way to practical considerations, and deadlines loom incessantly.**

## The art of packaging

Defining the layout of a Formula 1 car is a process of evaluating options, rejecting some and incorporating others. Those tasked with defining the concept do not have a free hand in this process, as many compromises must be made along the way. Theoretical ideals must invariably give way to practical considerations, and deadlines loom incessantly.

In race car design, the art of reconciling conflicting technical requirements to arrive at practical solutions is known as packaging.

Among the factors designers must consider are obtaining a center-of-gravity location conducive to good handling, attending to the engine's cooling requirements, ensuring the safety and comfort of the driver, and adhering to a set of dimensional restrictions imposed by international motorsport's governing body, FISA. In the process of achieving these and many other goals, designers will fail in their overall objective if the weight of the completed car appreciably exceeds FISA's stipulated lower limit of 1,114lb (505kg) in race trim: that is, with no fuel load, but with all other fluids aboard.

It will be legal, but uncompetitive.

Aside from the purely mechanical aspects, aerodynamic objectives hold much sway in contemporary Formula 1 car design. In fact, designers regularly subordinate the mechanical aspects to their aerodynamic goals.

Eric Broadley initiated the design process for the Lola BMS- Ferrari T93/30 and established the basic parameters, including the suspension characteristics. Rarely does a design concept originate totally from scratch, because that introduces too many unknown factors. Most Formula 1 cars are based on the previous year's concept, but incorporate a variety of improvements. It's a process of evolution, then, not revolution. In the case of the Lola BMS-Ferrari T93/30, Eric Broadley decided to base the chassis on that of Lola's 1993-specification Formula 3000 car, which was by this time at an advanced stage of design.

Broadley had most of his initial concept schemed on Lola Cars' Computer-Aided Design (CAD) system. He was able to use data on the Formula 3000 chassis that was already resident in the CAD system as a baseline. The single most significant departure from that concept was the need for a much-enlarged fuel capacity. Thus, the new Formula 1 car was, in essence, to be a stretched and deepened version of its Formula 3000 counterpart. To go the Grand Prix distance, it would require virtually double the fuel capacity of the Formula 3000 car – 60.7USgal (230ltr): an additional 29USgal (110ltr). As shall be seen, the fuel cell compartment is key to the entire concept. Its shape effectively defines the rest of the car.

As a general principle, the longer a car, the heavier it is. There tends to be an emphasis, therefore, on keeping the wheelbase as short as possible in Formula 1. In their efforts to reduce the wheelbase, however, designers have very little leeway, as the dimensions of most of the elements situated between the front and rear axles are either of a fixed size, or offer limited scope for reduction.

The regulations stipulate that the driver's feet must be behind the front axle, so a certain amount of space at the front of the car is already accounted for. Working

(6cm), to be precise. Compromise number one!

The engine is attached immediately aft of the fuel cell compartment, and is another mechanical element few race car designers have any influence over. When Eric Broadley's packaging exercise was in its infancy, an engine supplier had yet to be identified. Consequently, a set of baseline parameters were adopted, and Broadley's efforts were limited to deciding how a theoretical engine should be accommodated. Later, when it became clear that Ferrari's V12 unit would power the car, the parameters were altered accordingly.

Behind the engine lies the gearbox casing, which also houses an oil reservoir. Behind that, Broadley specified a version of Lola's all-new, transverse gearbox, which was by this time under development for the company's future Formula 3000 cars. The gearbox casing is another critical element, because

backwards from that, the driver is a 'mechanical' element not even the best designer can alter – and designers seldom know for certain who will occupy the cockpit when they are defining the car. Consequently, the cockpit tends to be sized to accommodate drivers with a average-to-tall physique. In Eric Broadley's case, that meant employing the cockpit parameters, with respect to length, of the Formula 3000 cars his company supplies to customers around the world. The basic Formula 3000-specification cockpit parameters were also altered with respect to width. Formula 1 races are of a considerably longer duration, and drivers therefore require a little more room in which to work.

It transpired that both of the drivers selected – Michele Alboreto and Luca Badoer – have compact physiques, so the cockpit, and thus the car itself, could have been made significantly shorter: 2.3in

*Soon after Eric Broadley had defined a basic concept for the Lola BMS-Ferrari T93/30, Mark Williams became involved. Being well-versed in implementing Broadley's visions, Mark was tasked with coordinating the design effort, and with undertaking certain design tasks himself.*

its length can be tailored to create the desired wheelbase. There is a direct correlation between wheelbase and weight distribution, because the shorter the wheelbase, the greater the effect of any weight transfer. In common with all the other Formula 1 car designers, Eric Broadley wished to transfer as much weight as possible forward onto the front tires, because it is an inescapable feature of any rear-engined configuration that the rear tires are burdened with most of the car's weight. Consequently, the car is less than ideally balanced. Furthermore, while the front tires need only exercise lateral grip, the rear tires must exert tractive effort as well, so anything that eases their workload is likely to improve performance.

FISA's new tire width regulation, due to come into force at the start of the 1993 season, promised to make transferring weight forward even more desirable. Under the new regulation, the maximum permissible width of all four tires was reduced from 18in to 15in (457mm to 381mm). Effectively, that meant that the maximum permissible width of the rear tires would be reduced by a proportionately greater amount than the maximum permissible width of the front tires, creating 'surplus' front tire capacity. Because of their higher workload, the rear tires are made as wide as the regulations permit, but the full permissible measure is never employed at the front (Goodyear, currently the sole supplier of tires in Formula 1, recommends a front tire width that will balance the rear tires: when it eventually came into being, the Lola BMS-Ferrari T93/30 was equipped with 11in (279mm) front rims).

In a nutshell, the upshot of the new regulation was the opportunity to place a greater load on the front tires, reducing the workload on the rear tires and opening a whole new area of performance gain.

Aside from the favorable effect on weight distribution, there are aerodynamic benefits to transferring weight onto the front tires. The more weight that's placed on the rear tires, the more rear downforce is required for cornering, which in turn incurs a greater amount of aerodynamic drag. It's preferable, therefore, to redistribute weight to the front and generate extra downforce with the front aerofoils, as this creates a better balance.

The desire to bring weight forward influenced every aspect of the concept-definition phase. As with the dimensional limitations outlined above, however, a combination of regulatory restrictions and mundane practicalities mean that there is precious little scope for the race car designer. Virtually every item with an appreciable mass has a predetermined location in the car. Because of the front axle ruling, the driver's position is fixed, which in turn fixes the position of the fuel (because the regulations prohibit fuel from being housed ahead of the driver), the engine is situated directly aft of the fuel cell, with the gearbox and oil reservoir immediately behind it.

At the car's extremities are the front and rear aerofoil ensembles. The rulemakers impose dimensional restrictions on these. FISA's *Yellow Book* of regulations states that the foremost extremity of the nose cone/front aerofoil ensemble must not extend more than 35.5in (90cm) beyond the front axle, and that the rear aerofoil ensemble must not extend more than 19.7in (50cm) aft of the rear axle. Ideally, the rear aerofoil ensemble would be mounted further out from the chassis, as that would increase its leverage, allowing it to be smaller, lighter, and more efficient aerodynamically.

It can be seen that a Formula 1 car is virtually packaged by the regulations, at least with respect to the main parameters, and designers have little leeway. The only items they can move to any appreciable degree are the ancillaries and the radiators. In a perfect (imaginary) world, one solution would be to build the car significantly underweight, then install ballast precisely where it's needed. Trouble is, the regulatory minimum weight limit is too low for this to be feasible.

In the case of the Lola BMS-Ferrari T93/30, the difficulties in building a car down to FISA's minimum weight limit were exacerbated by the fact that the weight of the Ferrari V12 engine, at 309lb (140kg) – about the same as a Formula 3000 engine – is high by Formula 1 standards. Using an engine weighing the same as those used in Formula 3000, Broadley's design team was faced with the challenge of producing a car that would be 88lb (40kg) lighter than its Formula 3000 counterpart, despite having a larger fuel cell and larger radiators.

On the 'plus' side of the equation, the Formula 1 regulations permit several weight-saving measures not permitted in Formula 3000. These include the use of titanium in the car's construction, and the use of carbon fiber brake discs.

It's obviously possible to build a Formula 1 down to the weight limit, because the top teams manage it – and, as a matter of fact, all of Lola's previous Formula 1 cars have been underweight when they've left the factory.

Modern Formula 1 cars are designed by groups of specialists, not by one visionary working alone. Nevertheless, one person is usually tasked with coordinating the efforts of the various specialists – taking decisions as to how the packaging process should evolve, and overseeing the detailed design work. Soon after Eric Broadley had defined a basic concept for the Lola BMS-Ferrari T93/30, Mark Williams became involved – his obligations to the design of the company's latest Formula 3000 car, the Lola T93/50, fulfilled. Being well-versed in implementing Broadley's visions, Mark was tasked with coordinating the design effort, and with undertaking certain design tasks himself.

There are four phases of race-car design: conceptual scheming, preliminary scheming, final scheming, and detailing. In order to add substance to Broadley's initial input, Mark Williams evolved preliminary schemes for the entire car, effectively, bar the chassis structure: namely, the four 'corners,' the drivetrain, the cooling and fuel systems, the engine and gearbox installation, and the mounting of the aerodynamic appendages, front and rear.

With many key aspects of the design already fixed, Mark had to adjust to a new working method. "I've had to work with certain fixed parameters and assume that there won't be any problems," he said while design work was in full flow, adding, "You just have to rely on your engineering expertise to work yourself out of a corner, if you suddenly find you're in one!"

Once Mark Williams became involved, the first priority was to oversee the bodywork styling, using a 1/3-scale clay model. At that stage in the proceedings, Lola's in-house aerodynamicists – both of them highly experienced – entered the project, being consulted as to the preferred bodywork shape, particularly with reference to the shape of the sidepods. Their previous assignments had been to the Lola T93/50 Formula 3000 car and the Lola T93/00 IndyCar respectively.

Later, when windtunnel testing got under way, the aerodynamicists would play a major role in defining the shape of the undertray, and the shape and siting of the front and rear aerofoil ensembles, which Broadley and Williams had decided should be derived from those already designed for Lola's Formula 3000 car.

By October 1992, a 1/3-scale windtunnel model had been constructed, and subjected to an initial series of windtunnel tests, allowing the concept to be assessed from an aerodynamic standpoint.

*"You just have to rely on your engineering expertise to work yourself out of a corner, if you suddenly find you're in one!"*

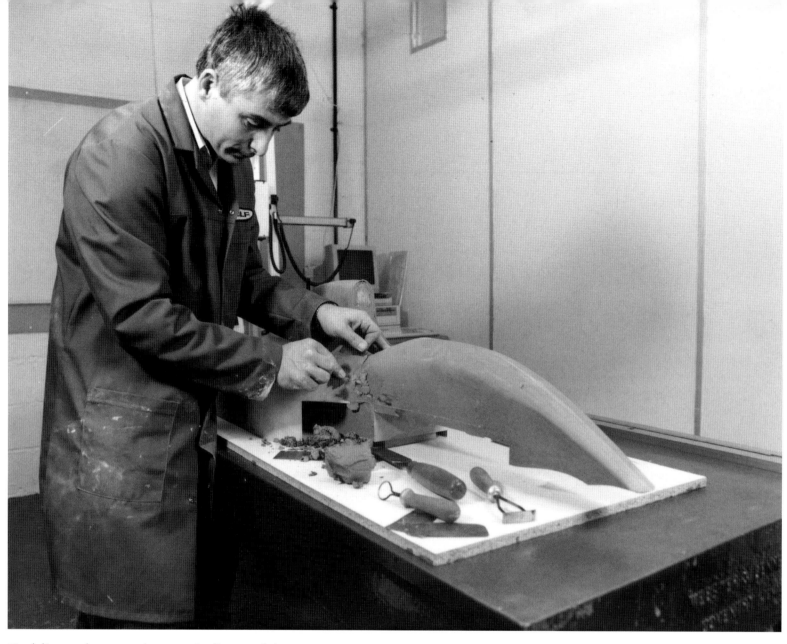

*To delineate the external contours of the car, the gaps between the Ureol foundation and the aluminium templates are 'fleshed out' with clay, as Lola's modelmaker is doing here. This is the art of styling – creating a three-dimensional form with windcheating compound curves that encompass all of the mechanical elements.*

## Styling model

Scale models play a crucial role in the design process. It's common for Formula 1 manufacturers to employ at least two types of models – a styling model and a windtunnel model – both built to the same scale. As with most aspects of race car design and construction, activities involving the two models are interrelated. In the interests of clarity, however, they are dealt with separately in this book.

The first time a new concept is expressed three-dimensionally is when the styling model is created. In Lola's case, a 1/3-scale styling model is built. This initial representation has three purposes. First, it allows the car's designers to visualize their con-cept more clearly. Then, when it has been refined to a certain point, it begins to function as a pattern from which much of the data required for the CAD system can be derived.

Finally, it serves as a pattern from which molds for the bodywork of the windtunnel model can be produced.

Under normal circumstances, with any new model in Lola's production race car range, the sizes and relative positions of the chassis, engine, gearbox and other constituent elements are fairly well defined before the styling model is built, and the previous year's car provides a baseline from which to work. There was a somewhat indistinct baseline for the

Formula 1 styling model, because although the concept was derived from the company's Formula 3000 car, it had to accommodate a different type of engine (the Ferrari V12), a new transverse gearbox, and a much greater fuel load.

Nevertheless, with time at a premium, certain key elements of the concept had to be frozen at a point when others remained unknown quantities.

Manufacturing lead times dictated the order in which the various elements were finalized. Scheduling called for the chassis structure – which usually has the longest lead time – to be finalized rapidly, so this was the first priority. The other elements would have to be blended in later, and any discrepancies resolved then.

As things turned out, once the chassis had been finalized, the bulk of the engine cover followed, then the nose cone was finalized, then the sidepods, and finally, the tail end of the engine cover where it shrouds the gearbox.

The foundation of the 1/3-scale styling model is made from a polyurethane-based pattern making material tradenamed Ureol – a Ciba-Geigy product that comes in slab form. The Ureol is cut to the required shape in Lola Composites' pattern shop, by a router commanded by software written in the CAD department. Unlike wood, Ureol is grainless, and therefore easier to work. It is also less prone to expansion and contraction than wood, being impervious to moisture.

In view of the ancestry of Lola's Formula 1 concept, the Ureol foundation for the 1/3-scale styling model was cut with the same CAD program employed for the company's Formula 3000 styling model. Some fundamental differences between the two concepts had already been identified, however, so a member of Lola Cars' modelmaking department was tasked with incorporating them. For example, the chassis of the Formula 1 car had to be longer and slightly deeper than that of the Formula 3000 car, in order to accommodate a larger fuel cell. Therefore, the Ureol foundation was extended in both length and depth.

To the miniature chassis, a 1/3-scale representation of the Ferrari V12 engine was added. Using dimensional data supplied by the Ferrari factory at Maranello, the scale engine was represented by three CAD-cut aluminium templates, positioned to correspond to its front, rear and upper (trumpet tray) extremities. A 1/3-scale gearbox was positioned behind that, again represented by CAD-cut aluminium templates.

The engine air intake duct was also defined. The basic shape was based on Lola's earlier, Ford V8-powered Formula 1 car (developed for the Larrousse team), but modified to account for the greater air mass flow requirements of the V12 Ferrari engine. Once again, Lola's CAD department generated a series of sectional representations of the intake duct, computer-cut from aluminium sheet.

All of these parametric representations were delivered to the model shop separately, in a sequence that reflected the designers' progress, so Hopkins had to make numerous alterations to the styling model as he laboriously pieced the three-dimensional jigsaw together over a period of several weeks. The various elements are assembled on a surface table to ensure that the model is 'true,' and that data derived from it at a later stage will be accurate.

To delineate the external contours of the car, the gaps between the Ureol foundation and the aluminium templates are 'fleshed out' with clay. This is the art of styling – creating a three-dimensional form with windcheating compound curves that encompass all of the mechanical elements. The modelmaker exercises this craft to particularly impressive effect when styling a miniature engine cover in clay. The engine cover of a Formula 1 car incorporates the air intake duct, sweeps down to hug the high points of the engine and the rear suspension, and extends back over the gearbox.

To reduce the modelmaker's workload, it is standard practice for only one half of the 1/3-scale representation to be styled with clay, because the opposite half, being symmetrically identical, does not have to be physically present for the next stage of the process – data-collection for the CAD system – to take place.

Styling the model is a somewhat subjective exercise, inasmuch as the modelmaker does not employ design drawings as he works the clay. There are, however, certain well-established principles to be observed: for example, keeping the bodywork as narrow as possible, in order to reduce aerodynamic drag. The modelmaker creates a profile he feels is correct, then members of the design team visit the model shop to suggest alterations. Clay is employed for styling models because it's easy to reprofile, add to, or remove, as the concept is progressively refined. The type of clay used is formulated specifically for the production of styling models in the automotive industry. It is very different to the clay used in ceramics: in terms of consistency, it's more akin to wax than conventional clay.

A variety of tools are used to work the clay, many of them fashioned by the modelmaker to suit his indi-

*Clay is employed for styling models because it's easy to reprofile, add to, or remove, as the concept is progressively refined.*

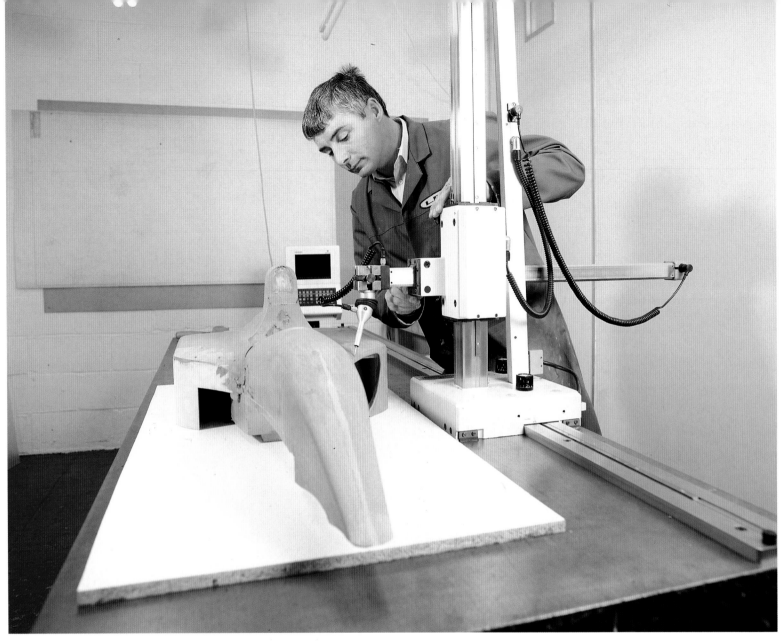

*Data can be derived from the styling model and transferred to the CAD system. This process is called digitizing, and involves plotting the precise spatial position of multiple points on the styling model's external surfaces by means of a Stiefelmayer three-dimensional measuring device linked to a pressure-sensitive probe.*

vidual methods. For the finishing touch, one of Lola's modelmakers uses an expired credit card – a Barclaycard, in fact – to create a surface sheen!

Among the more conventional tools employed are steel scrapers of assorted shapes, pieces of shim, hacksaw blades, and Surform ('cheese-grater') blades. Only scraping shapes the clay: it can't be smoothed into shape. Unlike the clay used in ceramics, automotive clay is worked dry. It's heated in a small oven prior to use, making it soft and pliable enough for working. When it cools back down to room temperature it becomes harder, but it never goes completely rock hard.

Once the basic body shape has been defined, a

proportionately scaled carbon fiber/aluminium rear aerofoil ensemble is borrowed from an earlier wind-tunnel model – it needn't be from a Formula 1 model – and mounted behind the styling model in the intended location. The designers find this useful, just as a rough guide, as it helps them to visualize the overall airflow across the car.

The clay model does not feature radiators, suspension elements or wheels – nor does it bear an undertray or rear diffuser – as the designers are only concerned with the styling of the bodywork at this stage. Suspension pickup points and wishbones *are* represented, however, as these are necessary to ensure that there'll be adequate bodywork

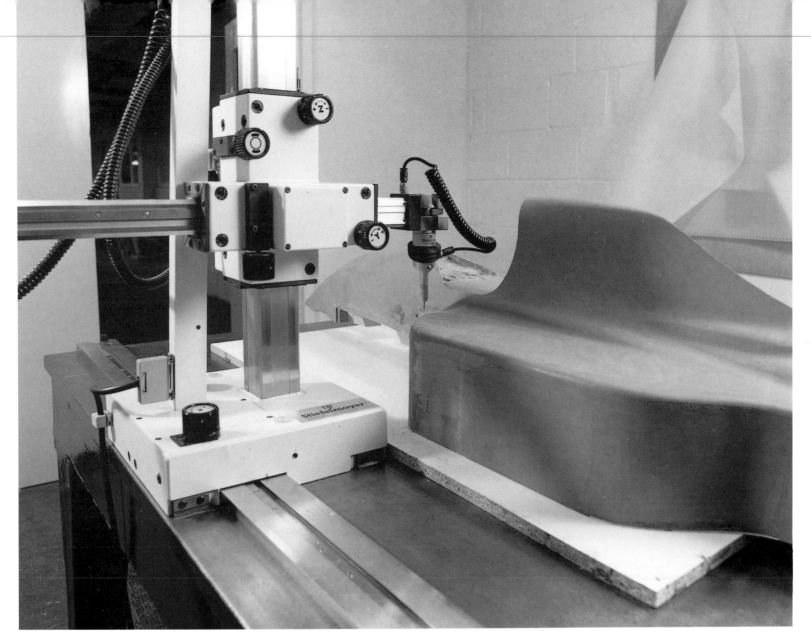

clearances: over the gearbox, for instance, where the rear suspension elements are mounted.

A host of changes are made to the styling model as the design effort progresses and the concept matures. To improve the aerodynamic efficiency of the Formula 1 package, the airbox was narrowed – but compensatory alterations had to be made to its shape, in order to ensure that the same air mass flow would be delivered to the engine. Other changes effected the cockpit surround. Clay had been added to increase the width of the original, Formula 3000-specification cockpit, because Grands Prix are run over much longer distances and drivers therefore require more room in which to work. The design-

ers subsequently calculated that the width could be reduced somewhat, so much of that clay was scraped away again.

The specification of the fuel cell compartment – situated directly aft of the cockpit – also changed fairly considerably, necessitating further alterations to the 1/3-scale styling model. After the initial concept had been defined in clay, the designers decided to reduce the wall thickness of the chassis in that region, in order to reduce the volume of the fuel cell compartment and make that part of the chassis narrower.

At a later stage in the design process, changes to the rear suspension configuration resulted in the

*The three-axis digitizer's controls are clearly visible from this angle.*

41

*The Stiefelmayer three-dimensional measuring device and the pressure-sensitive probe both operate through a Grundig MZ 1050 computer mounted alongside the surface table.*

aft end of the engine cover being reprofiled. Here, the bodywork has a finely chiselled appearance as it hugs the mechanical elements within. Under the original plan, there was going to be a single damper (monoshock) in the center, so appropriate templates were inserted in the model. When the designers subsequently elected to specify a *pair* of dampers, it was found that there would be insufficient clearance above the rear push rods.

The modelmaker: "A lot of chopping and changing takes place. The model is altered almost daily. It's worth it, though, because the more time that's spent on getting the clay model right, the less time that's needed on the CAD later. Also, the designers can get a better feel for the shape of the car from a three-dimensional clay model than they can from a flat CAD screen."

When the designers are satisfied that the styling model, or specific parts of it, accommodate all of the known parameters, data can be derived from it and transferred to the CAD system. This process is called digitizing, and involves plotting the precise spatial position of multiple points on the styling model's external surfaces by means of a Stiefelmayer three-dimensional measuring device linked to a pressure-sensitive probe, both of which operate through a Grundig MZ 1050 computer mounted alongside the surface table.

Only a slight touch is required to activate the digitizer and 'capture' a surface plot, at which point the device emits an audible and visual signal.

The digitizer records and stores hundreds of three-axis coordinates (X = longitudinal, Y = lateral, and Z = vertical), which are then relayed to the main computer in another part of the building to form the basis of CAD-generated data and graphics.

Some regions of the styling model are digitized several times as their shape is progressively refined. For example, a sidepod inlet, having been styled in clay, then digitized, might – at the designers' behest – be reprofiled and digitized once again. A case in point: during the first series of windtunnel tests, it was found that the radiator orientation and sizing had both to be altered, in order to provide sufficient engine cooling. Thus, the shape of the sidepods had to be changed. One half of the styling model was modified accordingly and redigitized, then the other half was modified, and a second set of molds produced from it. From these were molded the bodywork elements for what the design team considered to be the baseline windtunnel model.

Only the bodywork is digitized from a three-dimensional pattern in this way. The data required for detailed design of all of the other items, such as the elements that constitute the rear aerofoil ensemble, are either derived from hand-made drawings supplied by members of the design team, or are generated entirely on the CAD system.

42

## Computer-Aided Design (CAD)

A variety of advanced computer-based tools are used to assist in the design process. Computer-Aided Design (CAD) allows engineering drawings to be generated on-screen, then manipulated – for example, rotated or sectioned – to an almost unlimited extent in a fraction of the time it would take to create new sets of conventional drawings on paper.

When a CAD system is electronically linked to a cutting machine, or some other type of tool, a versatile extension of the capability – Computer-Aided Manufacture (CAM) – can be brought into play. Components modelled on-screen can be partially or wholly manufactured virtually independent of human intervention, saving time and money.

CAD/CAM input on the Lola BMS-Ferrari T93/30 was primarily focused on pattern making for the main carbon fiber and carbon fiber/Kevlar components: namely, the chassis structure (which includes the rollover hoop and the nose cone), the sidepods, the radiator ducts, the engine cover, the engine air intake duct, the undertray, and the front and rear aerofoil ensembles. In addition, the suspension coordinates were handled by the CAD system, together with the major mechanical elements that would lie in close proximity to the bodywork, so that clearances could be monitored. Chief among these were the engine/gearbox module, and certain elements of the front suspension.

Technical drawings for all of the mechanical elements were produced on paper. For all its capabilities, CAD will not supplant conventional drawing boards for some time to come.

Lola's CAD system generates three-dimensional wireframe graphic representations of components featuring curved surfaces. To conserve computer capacity, it's standard practice for only one half of the component to be displayed on the screen, as the other half is usually symmetrically identical. Work conducted on a CAD system is known as modelling. An initial set of point-coordinates defining the key dimensions of the component in question must be input before any modelling can take place. There are two methods of inputting point-coordinates: directly – via menus accessed on-screen with a light-pen – or indirectly, via devices known as digitizers, of which there are two basic types. One gathers data from two-dimensional sources, recording point-coordinates from a conventional paper drawing via an optical sighting system with crosshairs. The other gathers data from three-dimensional sources, recording point-coordinates from surface plots obtained from a scale clay styling model, a full-

sized pattern, or even an actual component, via a pressure-sensitive probe.

When the point-coordinates are input, the CAD system automatically connects them to form a series of parabolic lines. The CAD designer's first task is to move the points, where necessary, to create smooth curving lines. Then, in a process called surfacing, he mathematically generates an infinite series of flowlines that blend to define the component's three-dimensional form.

Once a component has been duly 'surfaced,' the whole gamut of design tasks can be undertaken on-screen. For example, the CAD system can generate a sectional representation of the component at any point (station) along its length. Typically, a sectional representation of the engine at the mounting points is produced for the benefit of the chassis designer.

Similarly, a sectional representation of the cylinder head can be generated: being the highest point on the engine, it has a direct influence on the shape of the bodywork aft of the cockpit.

One of the many advantages of a CAD system is its ability to reveal shortcomings in a paper drawing. Some components 'look right' in two-dimensional form, having been drawn conventionally on a board, but when they're visualized in what amounts to three-dimensional form on a CAD system, the same component is found to be deficient in some way. With CAD, there are no hiding places for such errors.

For this reason, it generally takes longer to produce a CAD model than a drawing rendered on paper, but at least then, problems that might only have become apparent at the pattern making stage – which is an expensive stage to discover them – are ironed out right at the start.

The CAD system prescribes the outer parameters of a component, so allowance must always be made for material thicknesses. In the case of the bodywork, which must offer sufficient clearances for all of the components it shrouds, this can be a complex process, because – unlike metal, which tends to have a uniform wall thickness – composite structures can have widely varying profiles, according to the layup requirements. Lola's CAD designers must therefore determine what the material thickness is at a given point by consulting the in-house composites engineer. The outer measurement is then offset to the appropriate extent, allowing clearances to be checked with confidence.

When CAD modelling has reached a satisfactory conclusion, the manufacturing (CAM) function

*One of the many advantages of a CAD system is its ability to reveal shortcomings in a paper drawing.*

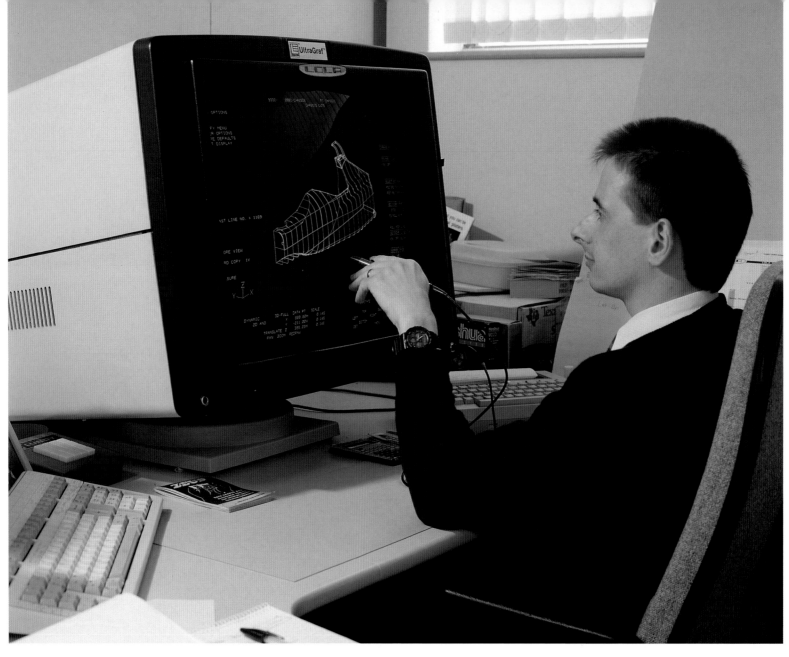

*Lola's CAD department manager is seen here using a light-pen to manipulate a wireframe representation of the chassis structure. Note that only one half of the structure is displayed on the screen, as the other half is symmetrically identical. This conserves computer capacity.*

can be engaged if required. At Lola Cars, the CAD designer, having written what is termed a Computer Numerical Control (CNC) program for the routing machine housed in Lola Composites' adjacent pattern shop, relays it to a central computer where it can be accessed by the router operator. Using the appropriate CNC program, the router then cuts slabs of Ureol to the required shape without human intervention.

To verify that the completed pattern faithfully reproduces the CAD system's graphic representation, data can be fed back from the pattern shop via a Stiefelmayer three-axis digitizer housed there.

Lola's CAD department employs software originally written for the Ford Motor Company, which is optimized for bodywork design. It's normally only available to contractors producing components for Ford vehicles, but Lola acquired it as part of a sponsorship deal.

There's a significant degree of cooperation between personnel generating drawings on conventional boards and personnel in the CAD department. If a designer working on paper at a board wishes to see a sectional representation of a component he's drawn, he can take it to the CAD room, where it will be digitized. Having gathered point-coordinates

in this manner, the CAD designer can quickly produce as many computer-generated sectional representations as his colleague requires.

When plotting point-coordinates in three dimensions, Lola's CAD system defines X as the longitudinal (front to back) plane, Y as the lateral (side to side) plane, and Z as the vertical plane. This applies to all of the race cars the company produces.

On the Lola BMS-Ferrari T93/30 specifically, the zero point for the X (longitudinal) and Y (lateral) coordinates was designated as the centerline of the front wheels, with positive values running aft, and negative values running forward. The bottom of

the chassis – at its interface with the undertray – was designated the zero point for the Z (vertical) coordinates, with positive values running upwards, and negative values running downwards.

To ensure compatibility throughout Lola's CAD/CAM process, the three-axis digitizer housed in the pattern shop, its 'little brother' in the model shop, and the two-axis digitizer housed in the CAD department, have the same system of reference.

CAD is a broad field that includes Finite Element Analysis (FEA): a method by which designers can analyze the loads acting on a structure, both at rest and in motion.

*This digitizer, housed in Lola's CAD department, gathers data from two-dimensional sources, recording point-coordinates from a conventional paper drawing via an optical sighting system with crosshairs. Here, a drawing of the Lola BMS-Ferrari T93/30's engine air intake duct is ready for digitizing.*

*Lola's in-house FEA specialist discusses a FEA-generated image with the company's composites engineer.*

## Finite Element Analysis (FEA)

Advances in computer technology, particularly with respect to miniaturization, spurred the development of new computer tools for aerospace applications, some of which have found a place in the motorsport industry. One of them is Finite Element Analysis (FEA), a computer-based method that enables skilled practitioners to analyze the structural characteristics of key components at the design stage with a high level of accuracy.

Any component's structural characteristics are infinitely complex, but by breaking a component down into a finite number of elements by computer, it becomes possible to analyze it accurately. The FEA specialist's first step is to simplify the structure as much as possible, removing features that don't contribute to the component's structural integrity. The simplified structure is then represented as either a two- or three-dimensional wireframe or solid model.

A computer-generated mesh is then superimposed through the model, enabling the FEA software to calculate the structural interactions within it by sim-

46

ply applying the basic principles of mechanics.

When analysis is conducted in a two-dimensional format, the mesh typically is composed of either triangular or rectangular elements. When analysis is conducted in a three-dimensional format, the mesh typically is composed of either brick-shaped elements or tetrahedrons.

By treating the component as if it could flex like a spring, rather than being a rigid structure, the FEA system then identifies and quantifies the loadings transmitted through each element of the mesh to its neighbors – and thus across the entire component – by measuring them at the theoretical joints (nodes) between the elements. A more comprehensive assessment can be made by interspersing an additional node (a mid-side node) between each of the primary nodes.

In the case of a two-dimensional analysis, a triangular mesh pattern produces three nodes per element (six if mid-side nodes are introduced), while rectangular mesh patterns produce four nodes per element (eight with mid-side nodes). Obviously, if a three-dimensional analysis is undertaken, more nodes are produced. A mesh composed of tetrahedrons produces ten nodes per element, while a mesh composed of brick-shaped elements generates twenty nodes per element.

The density of the mesh – where it is coarse and where it is refined – accords to the specialist's prior experience with comparable models: specifically, his knowledge of the structure, and the forces acting both upon and within it. There must be no discontinuity in the mesh, as the load path would then be interrupted, negating the test results.

Structural characteristics of a component can be analyzed in two distinctly different ways. In one, the subject is considered to be fixed in position, with loadings present, but not changing. This is known as static analysis. In the second, the subject is considered to be fixed in position, but with loads varying as a function of time. This is known as dynamic, or transient, analysis.

In both cases, theoretical loads are fed into the component at the point, or points, where the actual loads will be introduced, so that the effects can be assessed. A series of 'load cases' are then run through the computer program.

Since the component under analysis is but one part of the entire structure of the car, the FEA specialist must assume that all of the other parts are – to use the stress engineer's parlance – absolutely rigid, and that the component in question is assumed to be held rigidly at all of its interfaces with the other parts of

the car. The component under analysis can thus be isolated from the rest of the car, or the whole task would become impossibly complex.

In analyzing FEA data, race-car designers aren't just intent on limiting stress and preventing outright structural failure. More often than not, they're also concerned with the stiffness of the structure, as this is vital if the desired performance levels are to be attained. A suspension component, for example, must be made as stiff as possible without becoming overly bulky and heavy.

Having attained the desired stiffness, however, it's vital to check that the stresses inherent in the proposed structure are acceptable, as it doesn't always follow that limiting deformations (known as deflections) will also limit the stresses. This is particularly important when dealing with carbon fiber structures, because these are multi-layered, and the constituent fibers usually have a variety of orientations and may well possess different properties – creating stress patterns far more complex than those found in metallic structures. By attempting to introduce a high level of rigidity to a composite structure, a designer might be placing excessive stresses on the fibers, causing the structure to fail.

The FEA system is capable of identifying stress concentrations likely to result in structural failure, allowing designers to eliminate them. To facilitate such analysis, a comprehensive database of composite material properties – including failure criteria – must first reside in the FEA software. This is compiled over a long period of time by the FEA specialist, and represents a very considerable effort in itself.

No such database is required for steel, the properties and limitations of which are universally known, and therefore relatively easy to predict. Steel has a uniform structural composition – except when it's been the subject of a surface-hardening process, in which case the effects can be accounted for by the FEA specialist, by conducting his analysis in a slightly different manner.

Unlike metallic structures, which tend to fail progressively, the fibers in carbon-composite structures are prone to fail suddenly. Carbon is so brittle that it just snaps. When a failure occurs in some fibers, it transmits to the adjacent fibers, which in turn become overloaded and fail. Consequently, designers use FEA data to ensure that they stay well within the acceptable margins.

Once the analysis is completed, the results are displayed on the computer screen in graphical form, with values color-coded to aid interpretation. This is a major advance on early FEA systems, which pre-

*By attempting to introduce a high level of rigidity to a composite structure, a designer might be placing excessive stresses on the fibers, causing the structure to fail.*

sented data in a user-unfriendly, raw numerical form. In addition, the deformations of a component can be calculated in such a way that extremely small movements are artificially exaggerated on the screen, making it easier to isolate the areas where movement is taking place.

Aside from structural analysis, FEA can facilitate analysis of thermal behavior – typically, plotting temperature maps and analyzing heat-transfer characteristics – and fluid, vibrational and acoustical analysis.

Lola's FEA specialist is a young stress engineer who came to Huntingdon late in 1991 with limited industry experience, following a postgraduate course at Marquette University in Milwaukee, Wisconsin. Marquette has a burgeoning computer-aided engineering department.

Eager to work in the motorsport industry, he approached several American teams, without immediate success. He came to realize that with the amount of race-car design undertaken in the United States being really rather minimal, there was no requirement for an FEA specialist. He reasoned that applying to a Formula 1 team, or a production race-car manufacturer such as Lola – where higher levels of resources were deployed as a matter of course – might prove more fruitful.

One of the teams he had approached in the States was Newman-Haas, and someone there provided a referral to Lola, which happened to have just such a vacancy open at that time. Lola wanted to ensure that its nose cones and chassis structures passed the stringent crash tests FISA requires race car manufacturers to undertake. If a structure fails one of these tests, it's sometimes necessary to revise one or more of the molds, which is both expensive and time-consuming. It's far better to assure success by getting the lay-up 'right first time,' having predicted the outcome with FEA methods.

Lola added FEA to its existing CAD capability, and there is a high degree of compatibility. The company employs a standard commercial FEA software package called ANSYS, supplied by the American company Sevanson Analysis Systems.

A certain amount of generic data relating to dynamic performance was already available to Lola's FEA specialist when he started work on the Formula 1 project in August 1992, having been gathered by strain gauges fitted aboard a comparable Lola car: that year's Formula 3000 car, the T92/50. For example, a strain gauge had been mounted on a push rod to help assess how loadings varied as a function of time, or as an alternative, according to the car's position in a corner.

## Modus operandi

Lola is unique among Formula 1 constructors in that it manufactures a wide range of racing cars for customers competing in many different formulas across the world. Thus, members of the design team responsible for the Lola BMS-Ferrari T93/30 Formula 1 car also participated in the design of Lola's cars for the 1993 CART IndyCar Championship, and that year's national and international Formula 3000 championships, as well as the design of a car for the stillborn 1993 FIA Group C sports-prototype championship.

When Lola's directors took the decision to proceed with a new Formula 1 project, all of the company's design personnel were committed to generating the following year's range of production racing cars. As the Formula 1 design effort progressed, designers joined the project one by one as these commitments were fulfilled. In addition to Mark Williams, there were four other engineers involved in the design of the Lola BMS-Ferrari T93/30.

Many more designers were assigned to the Lola BMS-Ferrari T93/30 than would normally be assigned to one of Lola's production racing car programs, due to the fact that – following delays in securing a go-ahead for the venture – there was only half the time in which to do the job. Mark Williams divided the design work up and distributed it between them, assigning each designer a specific area of responsibility. Mark Williams then monitored their efforts and ensured that they were each informed of any design changes their colleagues made that might effect what they were doing.

The Formula 3000 design project was completed first, so most of those responsible for designing that car became available to join the Formula 1 design team – leaving just a skeleton team to deal with any difficulties that might arise during the production run, or technical problems encountered by Lola's customers after delivery. The first, having spent the best part of a year designing the first 'all-Lola' gearbox for an initial application in Formula 3000, was assigned the task of producing a version suitable for Formula 1 – and, of course, compatible with the Ferrari V12 engine.

The next designer to become available was assigned to what is termed the 'front cross-section': the front suspension, the front uprights, and the front brake installation. Having just undertaken the same task on Lola's Formula 3000 car, the requirements were fresh in his mind.

Yet another designer joined the Formula 1 pro-

A designer hard at work
on the Formula 1 project.

ject from the Formula 3000 design team. Since his prior commitment had caused him to join at a very late stage, it was logical that he be assigned the fuel system, as not all of the required information had been available during the initial stages of the design process.

In the same manner, members of the company's Group C (Lola T93/10) design team joined the Formula 1 effort. Although FISA had cancelled the Group C category soon after Lola unveiled the first T93/10, personnel responsible for that car were still working on a possible derivative for IMSA's GTP category, so they only became available for the Formula 1 project at a relatively late stage. One was assigned responsibility for the cockpit layout. When he had completed this work, he assisted with scheming the fuel system, as that had been deemed too big a task for one person to deal with unaided in the time available.

For his part, Mark Williams assumed specific responsibility for designing the drivetrain, the rear suspension configuration and mounting, the rear uprights, the rear brake installation, the engine cooling system (radiator plumbing and installation), and the mounting of the aerodynamic appendages.

Mark also undertook the design of those parts of the gearbox casing that would be receiving the rear suspension elements and the support structure for the rear aerofoil ensemble. It was therefore necessary for him to collaborate with the designer responsible for the gearbox. Similarly, design work on the front suspension had a direct bearing on design work on the dash bulkhead, because this carries the aft mounting points for the front wishbones: therefore, the two designers worked together.

Such liaisons are characteristic of the design process. With so many tasks being interrelated, it's essential that the designers cooperate. They must decide where the interfaces between the components they're responsible for lie, and reconcile the inevitable 'conflicts of interest.'

Aside from the five designers, three draughtsmen were assigned to 'detail' the Formula 1 car: another vital task. Two of them had just been freed from the Formula 3000 project, while the third had previously been engaged on the Group C/IMSA GTP project.

In addition, members of the CAD department played a key role in the design effort. Among their responsibilities was defining the bodywork 'splits,'

49

*This engineer joined the Formula 1 design team when his commitments to the design of Lola's latest Formula 3000 car were fulfilled.*

which Mark Williams monitored to ensure compatibility with the mechanical elements within.

Eric Broadley himself did not take a specific role beyond defining the initial concept. Mark Williams explained: "Eric doesn't tend to have a defined design task. He generally floats in and out – he's an overseer. Bear in mind that he's also got a company to run, so once he's got things rolling, he relies on me, with the other engineers, to then produce the car.

"With the Formula 1 project, because we still didn't have a big enough design staff to do the job in the time available, I did a lot of the actual drawing work myself – a large proportion of the car. I would probably not have done that much had we had another designer, because it would have been easier to give it to him and just supervise it. Then I could have kept more control on all the other elements of the project as they proceeded.

"Ideally, I would like to have been able to stand back a little bit and view the operation, and monitor all the jobs going through. That way, if any of the other designers get into a problem area and get stuck, I can give them the benefit of my experience, take it away, have a little design myself, give it them back and say, 'Look, I think this will sort your problem out.'

"Because we hadn't got another designer, Eric did a lot of that oversight work for me. We split the project management between us, into the areas we were most familiar with. I'm looking more at the mechanical side, while Eric's looking more at the chassis and bodywork. For example, having been involved with the initial layout – determining the length of the car – Eric already had a fair insight into the fuel system. Consequently, some of the little problems in that area he schemed-up in rough form, which one of the designers then picked up and finalized into hard lines."

The design effort was the first real test of the working relationship between the British and Italian sides of the Lola BMS-Ferrari partnership. Although the car was primarily a British-built product, it incorporated a certain amount of Italian-built hardware: the engine management system, the reserve tank oil system, the instrument panel – and, of course, the Ferrari V12 engine. As one might expect, there were extensive communications between England and Italy throughout the design phase, including visits by key personnel. One visitor much in evidence at Huntingdon was the team's German-born, Italian-domiciled Technical Director, Peter Tutzer.

Mike Blanchet, discussing the work-split as 1992 drew to a close, stressed that reciprocity was key to the Anglo-Italian partnership: "At the moment, we're tending to have their people come over here. That's logical at this stage, because all the design is being carried out over here, and all the people involved in the design are here, so it's easier to discuss technical matters here.

"But from the point-of-view of the political, commercial, administrative and other areas, we have to make the effort and go there – which we are doing, and will be doing in the future."

## The brief

Race cars are built to a brief, and Mark Williams was briefed by Eric Broadley to implement the Lola BMS-Ferrari T93/30 concept in a very short timeframe. Discussing the challenges facing him soon after design work got under way, Mark said: "Eric's brief is a difficult one. The car has got to be lightweight, yet inexpensive – and the two don't go together!

"Don't get me wrong, we're not trying to build a cheapskate car. It's just that we're trying to be sensible about it. We're looking at every component and asking whether we can use one we already possess – one that will do the job adequately. Maybe, then, at a later date, we can replace it with something lighter.

"That way, we can concentrate on designing the *new* components: the ones that don't exist yet.

"It's difficult, because it's tempting to redesign everything to try and have the ultimate parts, and you could easily get carried away. We simply didn't have the time. I've said to our people, if there's an existing component you can use that won't be detrimental to performance, use it.

"For example, we don't have wishbones and uprights, so that's the thing to concentrate on – and the fact that we've got pedals from all our other cars, *use them*. They might not be the lightest pedals that you could design, but they're very good production pedals. The bulk of our components are for Lola's range of production cars. When the cars go out of here, they don't come back, so they've got to be pretty sturdy. Obviously, the minimum weight limits are higher for IndyCars and the other categories, so we don't go to such exotic lengths to save weight. If you were optimizing the components for use in Formula 1, you would, of course.

"The most important thing is to have a couple of cars – plus a spare – down at Kyalami for the first race."

Mark Williams elaborated on the financial aspects of producing the new car: "The point about building the car inexpensively is this. If there *is* any surplus cash, we'd like to channel it directly into areas of performance gain: things that are going to improve our lap times a lot more than just redesigning something to make it a little more optimized – but a *lot* more expensive. You get to a point of diminishing returns.

"For example, you could adopt a blanket approach and say that you're going to make everything in titanium. But if you sit down and look at it objectively, you can see that you could actually make a particular component from aluminium, it'll be a darn sight cheaper, and you *can't measure* the benefit of making it out of titanium. If you had a blanket policy, you'd guarantee that the car would be light, but it wouldn't necessarily be any quicker – and it wouldn't be cheap. It's knowing where to draw the line.

"When we've got a finished car, we'll ask ourselves what we can do to make it better, and then do it if we've got the money."

> *"The most important thing is to have a couple of cars – plus a spare – down at Kyalami for the first race."*

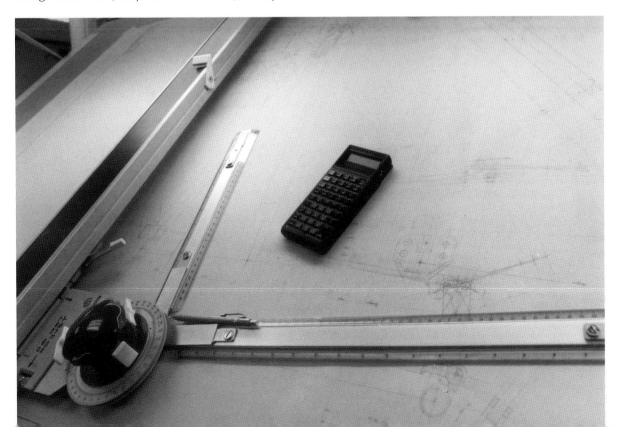

# CHAPTER

# 5

# Wind tunnel testing

*Not only are the external dimensions of the real car replicated, but also the panel-fit, internal layout, and material thicknesses.*

## The windtunnel model

To assess the aerodynamic performance of a race car, or specific parts of it – either before or after the car has actually been built – scale models are tested in a windtunnel. In the case of the Lola BMS-Ferrari T93/30, a 1/3-scale model underwent extensive windtunnel tests.

When the windtunnel model is built, technical drawings supersede the 'rule of thumb' interpretive methods employed to produce the styling model. Designed and fabricated almost totally in-house, Lola's windtunnel models are state-of-the-art. They are a huge advance on those used in the past, being highly representative of the real car. Not only are the external dimensions of the real car replicated, but also the panel-fit, internal layout, and material thicknesses. These refinements markedly improve the accuracy of test results.

In the past, windtunnel models were composed of solid wooden blocks. With today's hollow models, modifications can be carried out rapidly – an important point when one considers the enormous cost of windtunnel time. If the model has to be altered, modifications can usually be made there and then in the small workshop alongside the windtunnel. In the past, it was more laborious process. Solid-wood models had to be returned to the factory – or, if the modifications were particularly major – an entirely new model had to be made, and precious days lost as a consequence.

Creation of a new windtunnel model gets under way after the final round of digitizing the clay styling model has taken place. At this point, the styling model takes on its a new role – serving as a pattern for

the production of molds for the bodywork of the windtunnel model.

First, the clay is built up on the opposite half of the styling model, in a mirror-image of the digitized half. Then, a fine layer of aluminium foil is glued over the entire surface, to protect the clay from damage during the mold making process. A polyester-resin gel coat is applied, and when that has dried thoroughly, a conventional fiberglass hand lay-up is undertaken to produce the molds.

When the molds have cured, they are prised away from the clay pattern, which is put into temporary storage. The molds are given a polyester-resin gel coat, then layers of fiberglass are laid-up to produce the miniature bodywork elements.

By the same process, a separate fiberglass nose cone is produced.

The forward portions of the sidepods were also made separately, but were fashioned from Ureol. This was to facilitate experiments with a variety of different sidepod lengths and inlet shapes in the windtunnel. A total of three sets, each a different length, were produced.

All of the fiberglass and Ureol pieces are attached to a modular aluminium structure that serves as a backbone for the windtunnel model. This structure was mounted atop a 1/3-scale undertray, machined from a 1/2in (13mm) plate of aluminium. In keeping with FISA's Formula 1 regulations, the scale undertray had a flat underside, but was relieved on the inner surface to replicate the duct floors within the sidepods.

Three undertrays were produced for the windtunnel model – again, to facilitate experiments

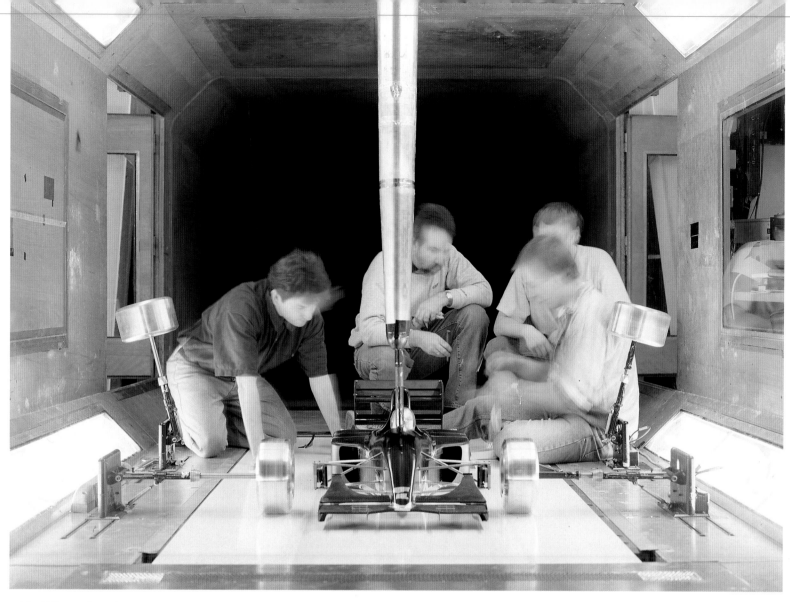

with different lengths.

Independent of the 1/3-scale styling model, a proportionately scaled pattern of the car's rear diffuser was crafted to a set of drawings. The rear diffuser is an upward-slanting aerodynamic device located immediately aft of the undertray, that acts in concert with it. The Lola BMS-Ferrari T93/30's rear diffuser was curvaceous, whereas most were composed of flat surfaces. Therefore, it was fashioned in clay, instead of being created by the more usual method of fabricating from sheet steel or aluminium. A mold was produced from this pattern, from which a 1/3-scale fiberglass diffuser was created for the first series of windtunnel tests.

Various modifications were found to be necessary once the model had been windtunnel-tested, including revisions to the diffuser shape. Consequently,

a new diffuser pattern was made. This pattern was subsequently digitized for the CAD system, then a mold was produced, from which a definitive carbon fiber diffuser was molded for the second series of windtunnel tests.

There was no need to modify this second pattern to account for further, subtler modifications to the rear diffuser shape as the windtunnel tests progressed, because modifications were limited to experimentation with various interchangeable fences and 'feet.'

Two substantial bolt-on brackets constitute the rear portion of the windtunnel model's backbone structure. They serve as mounting points for the rear suspension assemblies, and represent the volume occupied by the engine/gearbox module.

Four exquisitely detailed suspension assemblies

*Lola personnel systematically cajole performance gains from their miniature charge.*

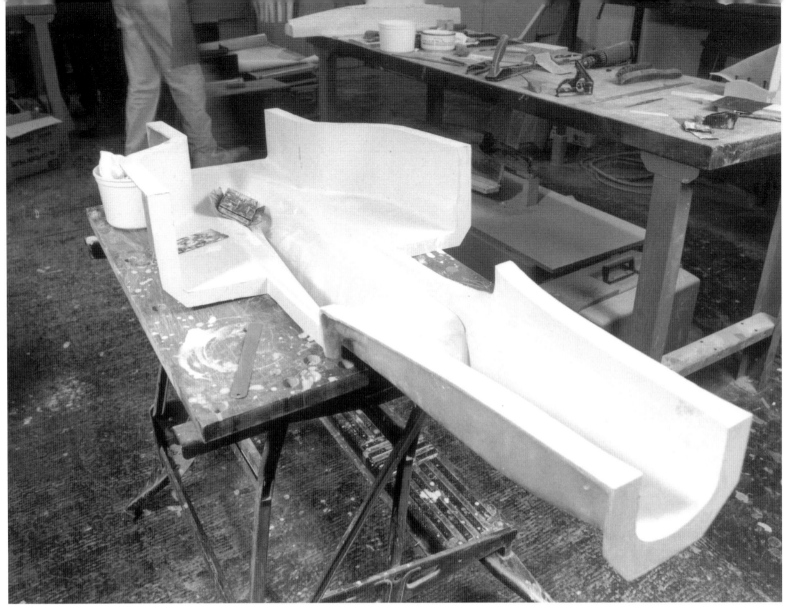

*Molds are produced from the clay styling model, from which fiberglass bodywork can be molded for the windtunnel model.*

were installed. Fabricated from machined pieces of aluminium, finished by hand, these incorporated rose joints so that they would articulate in a similar manner to those on the full-sized car.

The suspension design had yet to be finalized when the first set of windtunnel tests began, so the equivalent parts were borrowed from Lola's Formula 3000 windtunnel model as a time-saving measure – having been deemed sufficiently representative, from an aerodynamic standpoint, to support initial tests. Indeed, purpose-built Formula 1-specification suspension assemblies were not installed on the windtunnel model until several months later, by which time the first completed car had been racetrack tested.

Four scale wheel/tire units are also fabricated, from turned aluminium, and a ball race is installed in each of them to permit free rotation.

Aerofoil ensembles for the windtunnel model, front and rear, are crafted by Lola Composites. The front aerofoil is made entirely from carbon fiber, while the rear aerofoil ensemble is made predominantly from carbon fiber, but features aluminium endplates.

Replicas of the radiators are incorporated into the windtunnel model, to simulate the impeding effect of the radiator cores on the airflow passing through the sidepods. The miniature radiators have an aluminium honeycomb core, with layers of brass gauze glued to the front and rear surfaces with silicon adhesive. The number of layers can be varied to suit the degree of airflow impediment the designers wish to simulate. To prevent air escaping from

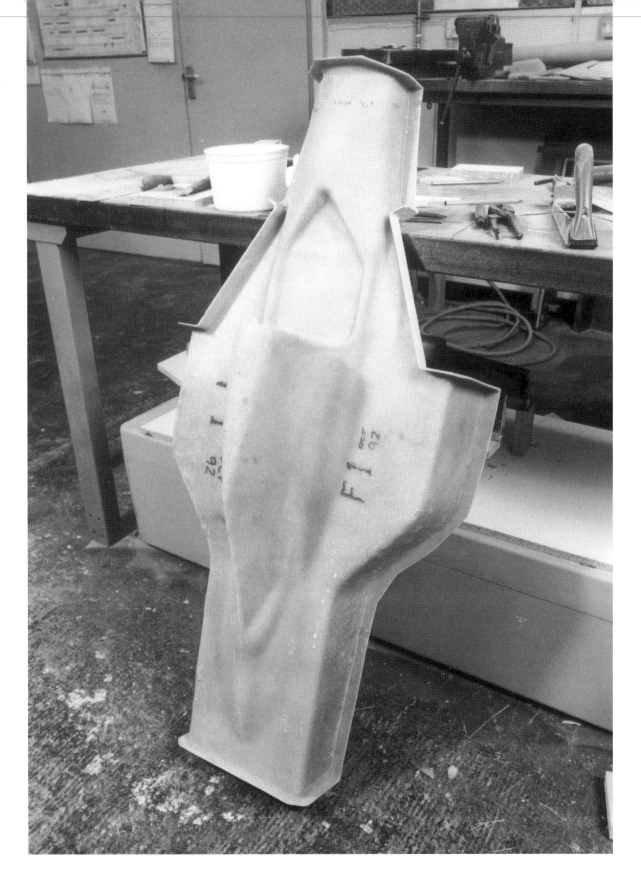

*The first bodywork mold for the windtunnel model – October 1992.*

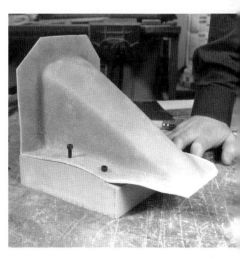

*By the same process, a separate mold is produced for the nose cone.*

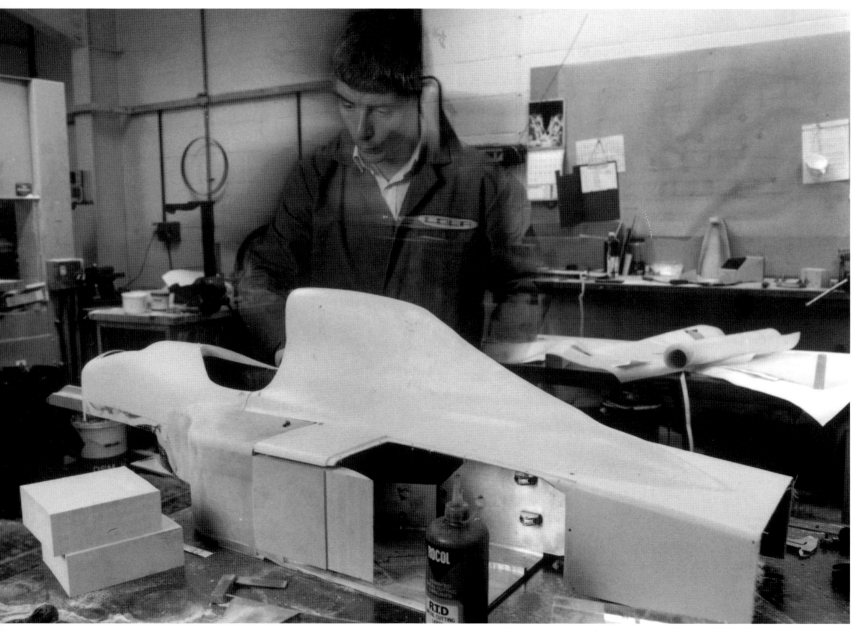

*Mounting the miniature bodywork elements on the windtunnel model.*

the edges, the miniature radiators are sealed with aluminium tape.

Dozens of flexible plastic tubes are inserted into the replica radiators, to sample the local air pressure at various points. The tubes are part of an elaborate pressure tapping system designed to measure the air-pressure differential between the front and rear surfaces of the radiators (a key design objective is to establish a lower pressure behind the radiator, in order to draw air through in the proper direction). The plastic tubes are connected to rigid stainless steel tubes – with 0.05in (1mm) internal diameters – protruding from an on-board measuring device known as a Scanivalve. This is linked to a transducer that converts the radiator pressure-differential plots into electrical signals. Data from the transducer are relayed to the computer in the windtunnel control room and stored for subsequent analysis.

A single, high-pressure tube is routed through

the model so that compressed air can be pumped into the rear diffuser region when required, to simulate the effect of the engine exhaust flow. This is a significant factor in determining the optimum diffuser shape. The compressed air is pumped out through two lengths of corrugated plastic piping. These not only carry the simulated exhaust flow, but also represent the impeding effect the exhaust pipe ensembles have on the airflow passing through the aft sidepod regions.

When the fiberglass and Ureol bodywork elements are attached to the aluminium backbone structure, a miniature driver's helmet is also installed. It is positioned to protrude just above the line of the bodywork, the way the real driver's helmet does, for even this has a measurable influence on the airflow.

Usually – though, in this particular case, not until much later – scale rear-view mirrors are also fitted.

During the course of windtunnel testing, the model undergoes numerous modifications. Interchangeable sections are taken along to be tested, the majority of which are fashioned from Ureol. Aside from the planned modifications, various impromptu alterations are implemented. Pieces are often sawn off and replaced with makeshift pieces fabricated in the adjacent workshop. For example, during the first series of windtunnel tests, a substantial area of fiberglass was cut from the aft regions of both sidepods and replaced with aluminium sections of a different length.

Clay is used to fill any gaps and streamline unevenly matched sections.

Whilst windtunnel testing is, for the most part, an exacting science, time constraints can occasionally force rather crude solutions. After several days of intensive testing, a windtunnel model often looks the worse for wear. This is one of the big advantages of mounting fiberglass bodywork elements on a modular backbone, because a new set of bodywork can be molded when the team returns to the factory, and a pristine model rapidly prepared for the next series of tests.

Windtunnel modelling is an on-going program, as 'variations on a theme' are windtunnel-tested throughout the season. Generally speaking, the clay styling model is not superseded. It continues to be employed as a pattern from which molds for modified bodywork shapes can be produced, then it forms the basis of the following year's styling model – initially as a conceptual interpretation, and subsequently as a subject of evolution.

Subtler modifications found to be beneficial during windtunnel testing rarely necessitate a complete new set of molds. It usually suffices to cut sections out of the existing molds and graft in new sections made from patterns of the localized areas.

Screen text:

Target Betz (mm)————————Normal Run——————Current—
74·0  71·1
Target Speed =35.0m/s    Time: 15h:41   BV=0.00V  Road=-0.0m/s  T=14C   P= 978mbar
—————Settings————            Results at——————Relative to-
Ride height map    = THE_MAP.RHM   Scaled to Fullsize    N/A
No of ride heights = 5000          Total Body Lift       N/A
No of samples/ride =    5 min(s)   Front Axle Lift       N/A
Estimated run time =  5 in map     Rear Axle Lift        N/A
Wheel drag reading = toggled off   %Front/Total          N/A
Pressure scanning  = False         Body Drag             N/A
GrafTool Data Toggle   False       L/D Body              N/A
Drive A Data Toggle    False       Front Wheel Drag      N/A
Model scale        = 33.333 %      Rear Wheel Drag
Ref fullsize speed = 150.0 mph     Total Car Drag
Current datum ride = 1.375/1.375   L/D (Total)
                                   Ride= 1.125/1.025  Run: 3027
Formula One                        Relative to-Run3025
Run tunnel upto speed... Press space bar when ready to acquire data.
Esc - Stop

*Data from the main strut-mounted load cell are fed to a computer in the control room, which overlooks the working section. Aerodynamicists engaged in race-car design tend to be interested in three parameters: downforce, drag and balance.*

## In the windtunnel

Aerodynamics are key to race car performance, and it is in the windtunnel that this facet is appraised. Most of the windtunnels employed for race car testing were originally developed for aeronautical research, and many are still used for this purpose. They are hired, usually for a 'block' of several consecutive days, for a fee of around $2,000 (£1,200) per day.

Because race car manufacturers wish to simulate the presence of the racetrack surface in their tests – something the aviation fraternity seldom requires – they hire windtunnels equipped with what's termed a 'moving ground.' A moving ground is an endless belt, akin to a conveyor belt, situated at floor level to simulate the racetrack surface passing beneath the car's wheels. To recreate real conditions as faithfully as possible, the belt moves at a corresponding speed to the airflow.

Moving ground facilities were first developed in the late-1950s and early-1960s, to assess the performance of jet-powered V/STOL (Vertical/Short

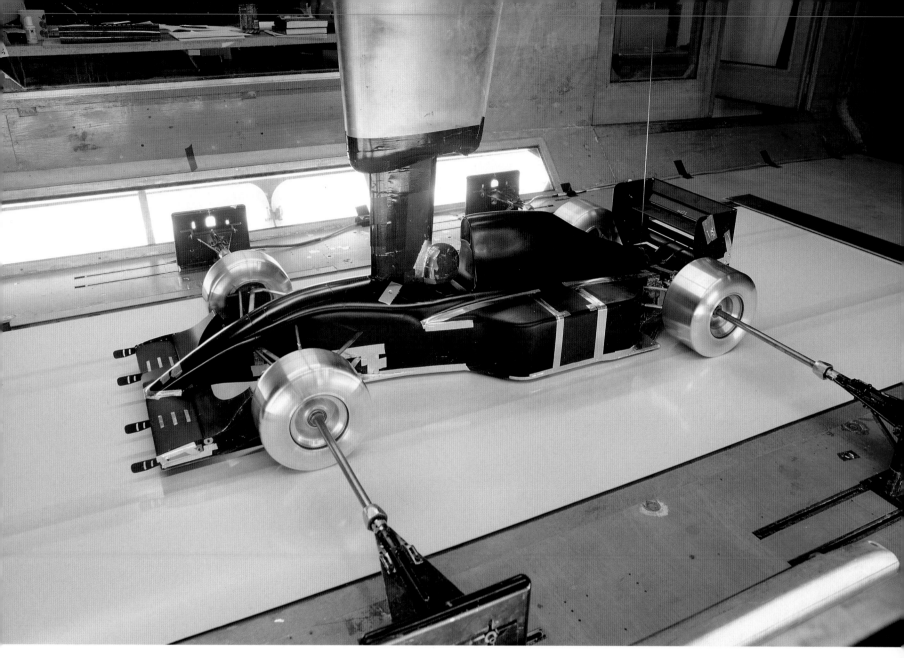

Take-Off and Landing) aircraft. The Royal Aircraft Establishment in Britain and NASA in the USA were among the early experimenters.

In terms of the sheer number of teams that use its facilities, the University of Southampton is the most prominent venue for Formula 1 windtunnel testing. There are, in fact, two windtunnels at Southampton. Interestingly, the larger of the two was originally modified for race-car testing with the active support of the Brabham team, in the days when Gordon Murray was its chief designer. Today, Jordan, Tyrrell, Larrousse, and the British-based technical arm of Ferrari conduct their windtunnel testing at Southampton.

McLaren uses the windtunnel operated by the National Maritime Institution at Teddington in Middlesex, while Benetton uses the Royal Aerospace (formerly Aircraft) Establishment's facility at Farnborough in Hampshire. Lola Cars undertakes its windtunnel testing in the facility operated by the College of Aeronautics at Cranfield Institute of Technology. Until fairly recently, Minardi and Footwork also tested at Cranfield, but Minardi now uses a windtunnel closer to home in Italy – where Ferrari also tests – while Footwork has established its own facility at its base near Milton Keynes,

*The 1/3-scale model of the Lola BMS-Ferrari T93/30 under test in the windtunnel at Cranfield, which has a working section 8ft (2.4m) wide by 6ft (1.8m) high. Note the vertical strut upon which the model is mounted. The wheels are supported on four horizontal struts and do not actually touch the model.*

Buckinghamshire.

Having previously conducted its windtunnel testing at Imperial College in London, Lotus acquired the windtunnel previously owned by the Williams team, which installed an even better one in its place. Ligier has its own facility in France, while Sauber undertakes windtunnel testing at its base in Switzerland.

There's much more to a windtunnel than first meets the eye. Photographs of windtunnels in operation – on the rare occasions when photography is permitted – usually show the windtunnel model suspended in the area known as the working section, but that is but one small part of the overall facility.

Out of sight, a huge fan impels the flow of air that passes over the model. The air column travels an appreciable distance to reach the working section, immediately upstream of which it is acceler-

ated as the walls close in from all sides to form what is termed the contraction nozzle. After exiting the working section, the airflow transits another leg of the windtunnel to be recirculated back through the fan.

The streamlined strut from which the windtunnel model is suspended is fixed to a steel platform above the roof of the working section. To isolate the model from any vibrations transmitted through the floor, this platform rests on a bed of cork and is a completely separate structure from that which supports the working section. The strut itself is part of a complex system that includes a load cell to measure the aerodynamic forces acting on the scale race car. Computer-controlled servos allow the model's pitch angle and ride height to be altered in a pre-programmed sequence while the windtunnel is in operation.

*A view looking forward towards the windtunnel's contraction nozzle. Note the device immediately in front of the leading edge of the moving ground, which siphons-off the boundary-layer – the thin layer of air that develops on the floor of the contraction nozzle, but doesn't occur under real racetrack conditions.*

Before this type of system was perfected – by the Pi company of Cambridge – the windtunnel had to be stopped after every run and the orientation of the model adjusted.

Data from the strut-mounted load cell are fed to a computer in the control room, which overlooks the working section. Aerodynamicists engaged in race-car design tend to be interested in three parameters: downforce, drag and balance. The latter is a function of the car's sensitivity to changes in pitch (when the car pitches nose-up under acceleration or nose-down under braking), and heave (when vertical translations – alterations to the ride height – occur as the car passes over undulations in the racetrack surface).

In the course of writing this book, the author spent a day in the Cranfield windtunnel watching a model of the Lola BMS-Ferrari T93/30 under test.

*The nine-bladed, variable-pitch, contrarotating fan at Cranfield is driven by a 500hp DC motor.*

There's much more to a windtunnel than first meets the eye – as this scale model, displayed at Cranfield, attests. Far upstream of the working section, a huge fan impels the flow of air that passes over the model. After exiting the working section, the airflow transits another leg of the windtunnel to be recirculated back through the fan.

Cranfield is situated near Newport Pagnell – the home of Aston Martin – a forty-five-minute drive south-west of Huntingdon. The windtunnel there was originally built to support aeronautical research conducted at the airfield site: the moving ground was installed much later.

Cranfield's windtunnel has a working section 8ft (2.4m) wide by 6ft (1.8m) high. The nine-bladed, variable-pitch, contrarotating fan that impels the airflow is driven by a 500hp DC motor. When Lola personnel test at Cranfield, they install the company's equivalent of the Pi strut system – which, they claim, is superior.

The moving ground at Cranfield is similar to those at the other facilities used by Formula 1 teams. While moving ground facilities operate on the same principle as a conveyor belt, they incorporates certain refinements to suit their specialized role. A device immediately in front of the belt's leading edge siphons off the boundary-layer – the thin layer of air that develops on the floor of the contraction nozzle, but doesn't occur under real racetrack conditions.

In common with comparable facilities, Cranfield's moving ground is borne on four rollers. There are two large rollers at floor level, and two smaller rollers

situated well below them. The large roller at the front of the working section freewheels, while the large roller at the back is driven. The front roller at the lower level 'floats,' so as to maintain the tension in the belt, while the one at the back can be adjusted to automatically 'steer' the belt.

Between the two large rollers and the two smaller rollers, immediately beneath the working section, is an elaborate suction system designed to keep the moving belt as flat as possible while the scale race car – with its ability to generate considerable downforce – does its best to lift it up. The suction system comprizes nine chambers corresponding to various points either directly beneath the windtunnel model, or at the sides of the moving belt, or at the front or rear of the belt. A manometer in the control room measures the suction level in each chamber. By activating a series of electrically operated butterfly valves, it is possible to regulate the air pressure in each of the chambers to keep the belt uniformly flat.

The only drawback to such a system is that friction between the belt and the surface upon which it runs – the plattern – induces a rapid accumulation of heat. To combat this, cold water (mixed

A close-up view of the windtunnel model, highlighting the front suspension elements, front wheels and front aerofoil ensembles. The four tabs extending from the leading edge of the front aerofoil are not representative of the full-sized car: they merely facilitate modifications to its profile.

*A manometer in the control room measures the suction level in each of the nine chambers directly beneath the moving ground. By activating a series of electrically operated butterfly valves, it is possible to regulate the air pressure in the chambers to keep the belt uniformly flat.*

*The scale wheel/tire units are supported by horizontal struts mounted on either side of the moving ground, and come into contact with the belt – rotating them at a proportionate speed. This arrangement allows a load cell to be fitted on each axle, so that the aerodynamic forces on the tires – drag in particular – can be measured.*

with an anti-icing agent) is circulated within the plattern.

It's usual to run the windtunnel at one speed – as fast as it will go. Generally speaking, the speed of the moving belt is the limiting factor in the performance of a windtunnel, rather than the speed at which the airflow can be impelled. The need to maintain a flat surface and limit wear are the key considerations. Typically, windtunnels are run at a speed of 165ft (50m) per second. The speed of the airflow/moving ground, and the forces measured, are not directly proportionate to the full-scale speed and forces, due to what are termed 'scaling effects.'

The computer employs a mathematical equation to scale the forces acting on the windtunnel model, then displays full-scale values.

The scale wheel/tire units are not actually fitted to the windtunnel model. Instead, they're positioned a fractional distance from the model, supported by horizontal struts mounted on either side of the moving ground, and come into contact with the belt – rotating them at a proportionate speed. This arrangement allows a load cell to be fitted on each axle, so that the aerodynamic forces on the tires – drag in particular – can be measured. Due to their large size, Formula 1 tires create appreciable drag.

Designers wish to assess how tire drag is influenced by changes that are made to the shape of the car.

Data acquired via the main strut-mounted load cell can be supplemented with visual evidence of the airflow's behavior around the scale model, if required, using a technique known as flow visualization – 'flow viz' for short. To visualize the *on-surface* airflow behavior, streams of a non-setting white paint (a paraffin-based emulsion) are flowed over the surface of the model. Alternatively, the *off-surface* airflow behavior can be visualized by passing a stream of white smoke over the model from a hand-held metal 'wand.'

If necessary, these activities can be documented photographically for later analysis. Windtunnel models tend to be painted flat black to aid identification of the paint or smoke patterns.

Flow visualization tends to be employed when aerodynamicists are engaged in conceptual work: it can be a good guide when investigating trends. When subtle alterations are made to a specific area of the car – a change to the height of the lower mainplane of the rear aerofoil ensemble, for example –

*Dozens of alternatively shaped 'bolt-on' pieces are taken to windtunnel test sessions: sidepod intakes, nose cones, aerofoils, and rear diffuser fences.*

the aerodynamicists can view the behavior of the airflow in that vicinity, then conduct a more detailed appraisal later on using the main strut-mounted load cell.

As with any technology-driven field, advances in windtunnel testing methods continue apace. Specialized equipment, now widely available commercially, can direct beams of laser light across the working section to measure spot velocities and turbulence levels at any point in the airflow without physically interfering with it. On the day of my visit to the Cranfield windtunnel, both of the aerodynamicists assigned to the Lola BMS-Ferrari T93/30 were in attendance. They were accompanied by two modelmakers. It was early-December, and the windtunnel had been booked for a week-long series of tests – the second spell in the windtunnel with the new Formula 1 concept.

While testing was under way, at least one of the aerodynamicists would join Cranfield's resident technician in monitoring activities from the control room, but the others tended to occupy the small workshop on the opposite side of the windtunnel. There, the two modelmakers fitted components and modified others at short notice, as and when required, reconfiguring the model to meet scheduled and unscheduled test requirements. They had brought with them dozens of alternatively shaped 'bolt-on' pieces – sidepod intakes, nose cones, aerofoils, and rear diffuser fences – with which to systematically cajoal performance gains from their miniature charge.

When the occasional difficulty arose, one or more of the assembled group would murmur the open-ing line of a well-known *Monty Python* tune to ease the tension. "Always look on the bright side of life...."

During the first series of windtunnel tests, it was essential to finalize the shape the chassis, including the sidepods. Defining the later meant finalizing the radiator layout, so that the CAD designers could complete their detailed models of these elements, allowing pattern-making to get under way. The process of reaching design solutions is known as 'optimization': baseline configurations are evaluated, adjusted and eventually optimized.

After some major 'chopping and changing' had taken place, the radiator layout was defined, and the optimum length and height of the sidepods were determined, and their basic shape delineated.

That was all that was needed at this stage. The undertray length and the rear diffuser shape remained fluid, but there was time to finalize these later.

After the first series of windtunnel tests, the by-now somewhat dishevelled bodywork was removed from the model and replaced with bodywork that reflected the various changes. When the restyled model was taken to Cranfield for the second series of windtunnel tests, a marked improvement was noted. The car generated more downforce. Design chief Mark Williams was obviously delighted: "We've made a gain. That's looking positive, because we wanted to find a bit more performance. We weren't happy with what we got from the first test, and we're actually now more on target for what we expected to see."

Those engaged in windtunnel testing a concept due for imminent production have rapidly diminishing options. When they went into the windtunnel for the second time, the designers knew they couldn't change the chassis or sidepods, because these were now committed to production. By the middle of the second series of tests, they had no options at all, because that was when the deadline fell for optimization of the undertray length, the rear diffuser shape, and the front and rear aerofoil configurations.

Up until that date, work conducted in the windtunnel had been hand-in-glove with the production process. Now, the windtunnel program would have no influence on the specification of the three cars at their first race meeting: the South African Grand Prix at Kyalami. The remaining half of that second series of windtunnel tests was therefore spent evaluating refinements that would appear after the first race: alternative aerofoil configurations and suchlike.

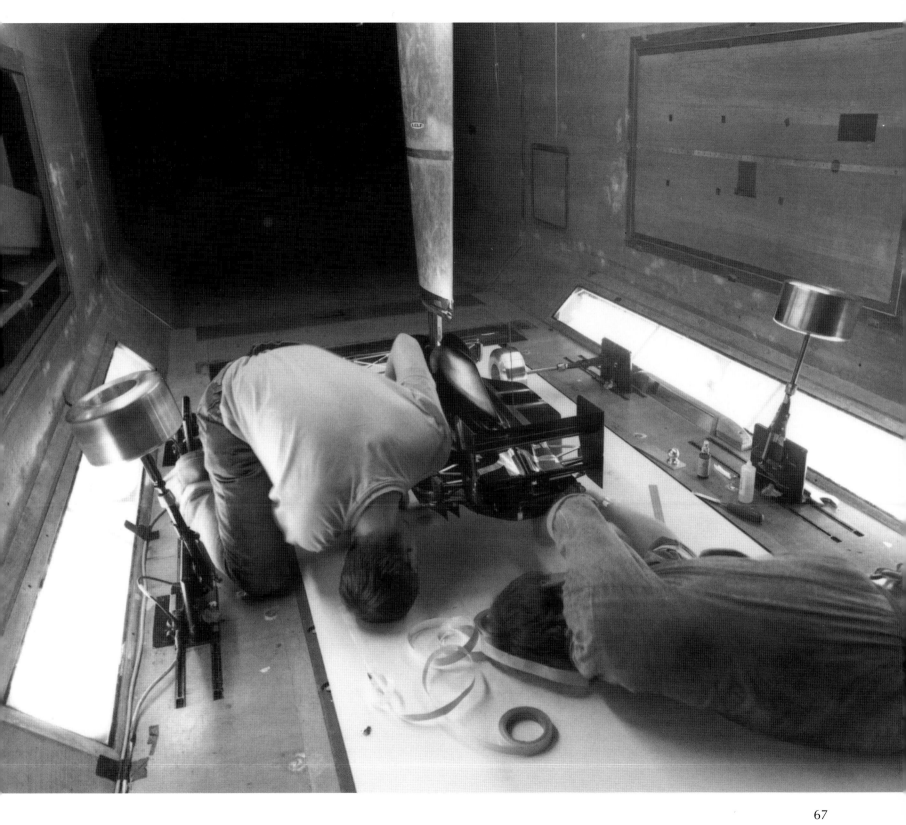

# CHAPTER

# 6

# The chassis

**One fundamental design objective is to build in sufficient stiffness to prevent the chassis flexing under cornering loads, and thereby becoming an unpredictable variable in the car's handling.**

## Design requirements

The chassis, or monocoque tub, is the central structural element of a Formula 1 car. Virtually all of the other load bearing elements are attached directly to it. It goes without saying that the chassis must be capable of sustaining a diverse variety of loads, and that some of the structural requirements conflict. Before examining the way in which the chassis of a modern Formula 1 car is manufactured, it is worth considering these diverse structural requirements and the materials designers employ to fulfil them. One fundamental design objective is to build in sufficient stiffness to prevent the chassis flexing under cornering loads, and thereby becoming an unpredictable variable in the car's handling. Here, the requirement is for both torsional stiffness (a resistance to twisting loads) and beam stiffness (a resistance to either lateral or longitudinal bending loads). The top Formula 1 designers have set high standards of torsional rigidity, which others must emulate if they're to be competitive. The target figure is 30,000lb ft/deg (40,680Nm/deg): meaning, if a 3,000lb (1,360kg) weight was placed at one end of a 10ft (3m) long lever applied at an angle of ninety degrees to the extreme front or extreme rear of the chassis, the tub would twist only one degree over its entire length.

Another fundamental design objective is to build in sufficient impact resistance. The chassis must be resilient enough to protect the driver in the event of an accident: furthermore, its ability to absorb energy must be demonstrated to FISA's satisfaction in a rigorous series of crash tests.

Carbon fiber is employed extensively in the construction of Formula 1 chassis structures. It lends itself well to the high performance requirements of Formula 1. Unlike steel, which has a uniform, homogenized (isotropic) constitution, carbon fiber has a biased (non-isotropic) constitution. Therefore, by positioning pieces of carbon fiber so the fibers are oriented in particular directions, it's possible to direct loads across the chassis as required and thereby dissipate them.

For example, it may be necessary to distribute incoming loads to a part of the chassis where reinforcements lie. In that case, multiple layers of carbon fiber oriented so that the fibers run in that direction, transfers the loads to the desired region. Conversely, multiple layers oriented so the fibers run in a variety of directions, distributes loads over a wide area. The specific orientation of the fibers depends upon whether the loads being dealt with in that region are torsional, compressive, or tensile. Similarly, the types of carbon fiber specified for each region, layer on layer, vary according to the nature of the loads that must be countered.

The carbon fiber materials employed by Lola BMS-Ferrari and the other Formula 1 teams are of the type known as carbon-composites. The term composite is applied to them because they are a composite of two elements: the fibers themselves and a pre-impregnated epoxy resin. Pre-impregnating the fibers ensures that the resin is evenly distributed, imparting a consistent structural performance. In most cases, the resin is specially formulated to the team's requirements and accounts for 40-50 percent of the carbon fiber's total weight.

Carbon fiber pre-impregnated with resin is referred

to as pre-preg.

The multi-ply carbon fiber construction is only part of the total structure. The carbon fiber layers form two skins that sandwich an aluminium honeycomb core material to produce a structure of immense rigidity and strength – and, vitally, low weight, for structural requirements must always be reconciled with the need to contain weight. Designers are constantly mindful of FISA's 1,114lb (505kg) minimum weight limit for Formula 1 cars in race trim. It is a testimony to their abilities, and to the excep-

tional properties of the carbon-composite/aluminium honeycomb construction method, that a bare Formula 1 chassis typically weighs just 80lb (35kg), yet is capable of transferring 750bhp to the racetrack and withstanding at least two tons of aerodynamic downforce.

There's a potential conflict between the need for structural stiffness and the need for impact resistance. With any carbon fiber material, the more stiffness it offers, the less resilience it has. Some Formula 1 teams employ what are termed high modulus car-

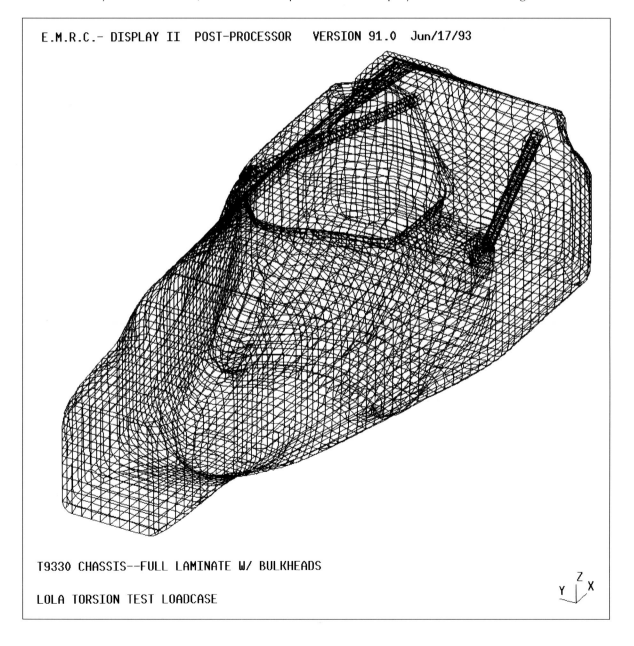

E.M.R.C.- DISPLAY II  POST-PROCESSOR    VERSION 91.0  Jun/17/93

T9330 CHASSIS--FULL LAMINATE W/ BULKHEADS

LOLA TORSION TEST LOADCASE

*A Finite Element Analysis (FEA) model of the Lola BMS-Ferrari T93/30's chassis, with a mesh of quadrilaterals superimposed for the purposes of structural analysis. The seat back is just visible, through the cockpit opening, as are the two engine mount bracing tubes. The other two bulkheads – the dash bulkhead and the rocker bulkhead – are considered to be present, but they are not shown, being represented mathematically only.*

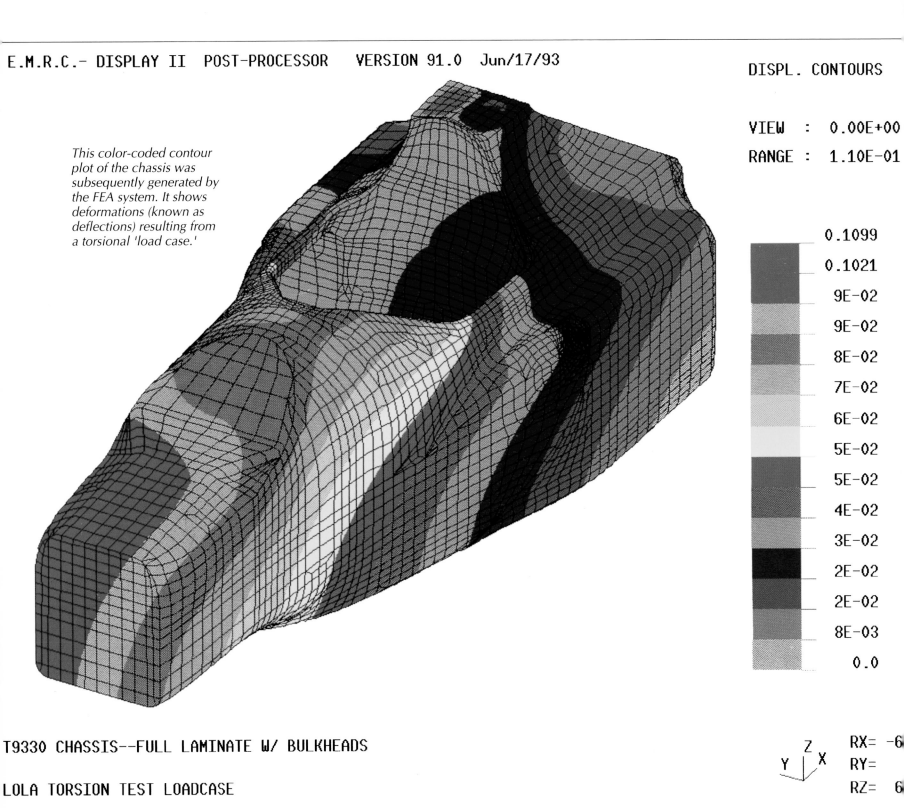

E.M.R.C.- DISPLAY II POST-PROCESSOR    VERSION 91.0   Jun/17/93

DISPL. CONTOURS

VIEW :  0.00E+00

RANGE :  1.10E-01

*This color-coded contour plot of the chassis was subsequently generated by the FEA system. It shows deformations (known as deflections) resulting from a torsional 'load case.'*

0.1099

0.1021

9E-02

9E-02

8E-02

7E-02

6E-02

5E-02

5E-02

4E-02

3E-02

2E-02

2E-02

8E-03

0.0

T9330 CHASSIS--FULL LAMINATE W/ BULKHEADS

LOLA TORSION TEST LOADCASE

RX= -6

RY=

RZ= 6

bon fibers, which offer unparalleled stiffness. The dividing line between stiffness and brittleness is a fine one, however, and Lola's policy is not to employ high modulus carbon fibers – even though these other teams pass FISA's mandatory crash tests with them.

Whether a designer eschews high modulus carbon fibers or embraces them, he can ease the conflict between the need for structural stiffness and the need for impact resistance by conceiving an effective *shape* for the chassis: a shape with smooth flowing lines that spread loads evenly, rather than sharp corners that concentrate them. However, the composite engineer's task is complicated by the fact that structural ideals are frequently overridden by the designers' aerodynamic and mechanical requirements. The best example of this is the stepped nose arrangement evolved several years ago to improve the aerodynamic efficiency of the front aerofoils and the undertray. From the structural standpoint, the stepped nose presents a huge challenge, because fulfilling FISA's frontal impact requirements would be much simpler – and the resulting car appreciably lighter – with a conventional nose arrangement in which the load paths are essentially straight.

At Lola Cars, achieving a balance between the stiffness requirements and the resilience requirements with a structure of the lowest possible weight is the responsibility of the in-house composites engineer. Following initial studies and windtunnel testing, the designers present the composites engineer with their ideal shape from the mechanical and aerodynamic standpoints, and he must reconcile their requirements with what he deems practical from a structural standpoint.

If the composites engineer objects strongly to a particular aspect of a proposed concept, it's usually because past experience tells him that achieving the necessary blend of stiffness and resilience will incur an unacceptable weight penalty. In that case, he must generate a revised concept in which the offending feature is amended to a form he deems practical, but which parallels the original concept in every other respect. Aerodynamic factors are the most frequent source of demands on the structural status quo, so if the feature in question was one introduced to aid aerodynamic efficiency, the composites engineer's revised concept must be returned to the windtunnel to ensure that no other aspects of the design have been compromized.

Making extensive use of Finite Element Analysis (FEA) techniques, the composites engineer then determines precisely what form the carbon-composite layup should take, in respect to both fiber orientation and quantity. He analyzes the structural characteristics of the chassis under cornering loads and assesses the effect of adding a further carbon fiber ply to a particular region in a particular orientation, then taking it away again, thereby quantifying its contribution to the overall structural performance. Generally speaking, his aim is to achieve his structural objectives with the minimum amount of material, thereby saving weight. The composites engineer must also strive to make his proposed layup a practical one: "It's no good designing something that can't be built".

High performance carbon fibers are very expensive. In Lola's traditional role of manufacturing production race cars, cost factors must be taken into account. However, cost tends not to be a constraining factor in Formula 1, where performance is the overriding criterion.

It's impossible, within the onerous weight constraints, to resolve the diverse structural requirements using the multi-layered carbon fiber/aluminium honeycomb sandwich construction alone. The composites engineer must therefore devise a system of internal reinforcements. Three bulkheads were incorporated into the chassis of the Lola BMS-Ferrari T93/30 to enhance torsional rigidity: a seat back, a dash bulkhead and a rocker bulkhead. In addition – perhaps uniquely – two sturdy bracing tubes were installed to help disperse the fore and aft loads fed into the chassis from the upper engine mounts, enhancing beam stiffness.

Local reinforcements must be provided to counter concentrated loads exerted where retention bolts for the front damper mounts and wishbone mounts, the sidepods, and other fittings will pass through the carbon-composite/aluminium honeycomb structure. Known as inserts, these reinforcements are pre-shaped pieces of high density material inset into the aluminium honeycomb core. Without them, the bolts would simply displace under the loads acting upon them, crushing the honeycomb material – which has a high resistance to end-on loads, but is susceptible to loads exerted at lateral or oblique angles – and fracturing the carbon fiber skins. The composites engineer must decide where inserts are required and determine the precise form they'll take. As one would expect, each insert must possess a compressive strength at least equal to the forces applied by the bolt that will pass through it. The majority are made from a laminated polypropylene material tradenamed Tufnol, while others are produced from carbon fiber or fashioned from solid aluminium.

*There's a potential conflict between the need for structural stiffness and the need for impact resistance.*

*One by one, the Ureol slabs are positioned beneath the router head on an air-bearing surface table, then firmly secured to prevent any slippage while cutting is under way.*

## Pattern making

Due to the long lead times involved, the chassis is usually the first part of the car to be built. It would be impractical, from both the production and operational standpoints, for the chassis to be constructed in one piece. Most chassis are composed of eight carbon-composite elements: an upper half, a lower half, the rollover hoop, the nose cone body, the nose cone tip, the damper hatch (a fairing that covers the inboard components of the front suspension), the seat back and the dash bulkhead.

All of these elements are known as panels.

Before construction can begin, eight patterns must be made: one for each panel. A mold is produced from each of these eight patterns, and from those the panels themselves are produced.

At Lola Composites, all eight patterns are computer-cut from slabs of Ureol and hand finished. The patterns for the nose cone tip and the dash bulkhead can each be hewn from a single slab of Ureol, but the depth of the other chassis patterns exceeds that of a single slab, so these are composed of several layers of Ureol slab stacked one atop the other.

The pattern making process marks the transition from CAD (Computer-Aided Design) to CAM (Computer-Aided Manufacture). The appropriate

*Extra pieces of Ureol have been glued onto the top surface of this slab, permitting raised features to be profiled.*

CNC (Computer Numerical Control) program from the CAD system is accessed by a computer-controlled routing machine housed in a small workshop adjacent to the pattern shop at Lola Composites' Glebe Road premises. Commanded by that program, the router machines the Ureol slabs to the required shape.

One by one, the slabs are positioned beneath the router head on an air-bearing surface table, then firmly secured to prevent any slippage while cutting is under way. As well as profiling each slab to conform to the three-dimensional shape prescribed for the pattern – matching them, when necessary, to those that will lie above and/or below them – the CAD-driven router drills a series of holes through which lengths of steel dowel will pass when the multi-layered patterns are pieced together later.

When all of the pieces that constitute a multi-layered pattern have been cut, a 'dry run' is conducted in the main pattern shop. The lower half of the chassis is usually the first of these patterns to undergo this process. The pieces are stacked on 1/4in (6mm) diameter steel dowels protruding from a large surface table. Each of the pieces are numbered to ensure that they are stacked in the correct order.

The 'dry run' is undertaken partly to ascertain

*The pattern making process marks the transition from CAD (Computer-Aided Design) to CAM (Computer-Aided Manufacture). The appropriate CNC (Computer Numerical Control) program from the CAD system is accessed by the routing machine. Commanded by that program, the router machines the Ureol slabs to the required shape.*

the required lengths of the dowels, so that they can be cut accordingly, and partly to ensure that all of the drill holes are in alignment. If the 'dry run' has proved successful, the pieces are disassembled, then restacked once more – but this time with a coating of epoxy adhesive applied between each layer. When the final piece is in position, the top of each drill hole is filled with a plug of Ureol.

Multi-layered chassis patterns are then taken back to the Glebe Road site, where any large internal cavities are filled with an expanding foam – again, to ensure that pockets of trapped air don't make their way to the surface later. The task is undertaken with an equal mix of two agents that, shortly after contact, create a foam that expands to fill the void, then hardens.

*Close-up view of the control and monitoring console for the routing machine.*

Cutting under way. As well as profiling each slab to conform to the three-dimensional shape prescribed for the pattern – matching them, when necessary, to those that will lie above and/or below them – the CAD-driven router drills a series of holes through which lengths of steel dowel will pass when the multi-layered patterns are pieced together later.

*A typical chassis pattern layer after profiling. The router leaves a border that is broken away before stacking.*

When all of the pieces that constitute a multi-layered pattern have been cut, a 'dry run' is conducted in the main pattern shop. The pieces are stacked on 1/4in (6mm) diameter steel dowels protruding from a large surface table. Each of the pieces are numbered to ensure that they are stacked in the correct order.

79

The patterns are sprayed with a coat of a gray-colored polyester spray filler paint. When dry, this shines – highlighting any uneven areas, which can then be hand flatted to a smooth finish.

When adjoining patterns are ready, they are bolted together temporarily so that the entire external surface area can be hand sanded with wet-or-dry paper, removing the machining marks left by the router and ensuring that the joints between the patterns are absolutely smooth: this is known as shaping through. Hand sanding also 'assists' the lines to flow, because the machine – being a machine –

does not always interpret the perfect line.

Particular care must be taken to ensure that the nose cone pattern is accurately aligned with the upper and lower chassis patterns, as even a minute misalignment at this stage will result in the front aerofoil mainplane being badly out of kilter when the car is finally assembled.

The patterns are separated following shaping

through, but certain regions may still undergo minor reprofiling with wet-or-dry paper – provided the regions close to the edges are not altered, as their shapes would then no longer correspond to the edges of the neighboring patterns.

When the shapes of the patterns are deemed to be correct, they are sprayed with a coat of a gray-colored polyester spray filler paint. This dries at room temperature and, when dry, shines – highlighting any uneven areas, which can then be hand flatted to a smooth finish.

Finally, each pattern is coated with a yellow-colored epoxy paint that protects the surface against chemical attack from the resins used in the mold making process. The patterns are ovened at 40degC (105degF) for one hour to harden the paint and

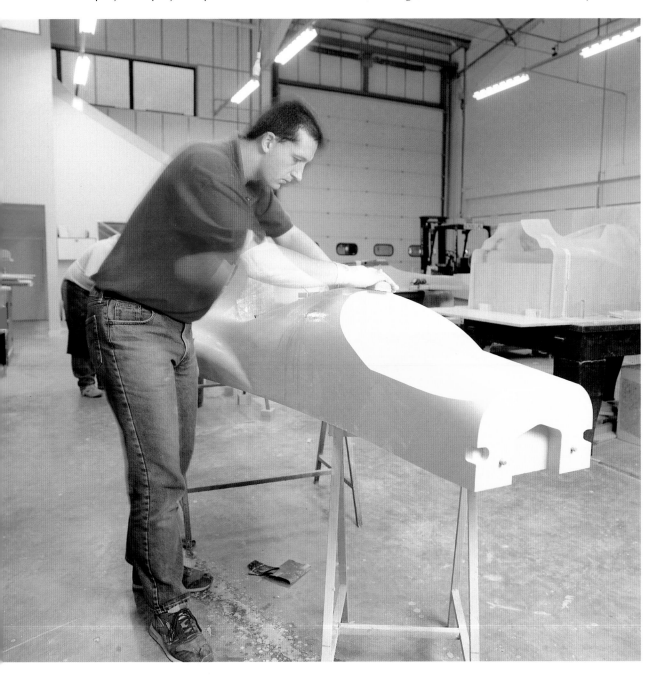

*The completed patterns are hand sanded with very fine (1000-grit) wet-or-dry paper. This is the pattern for the upper half of the chassis.*

Clearly visible in this photo are the joints between the various pattern elements: the upper and lower chassis halves, the damper hatch (a fairing that covers the inboard components of the front suspension), the nose cone body, and the nose cone tip.

After cleaning with an air line (pictured), each pattern is coated with a yellow-colored epoxy paint that protects the surface against chemical attack from the resins used in the mold making process, then ovened.

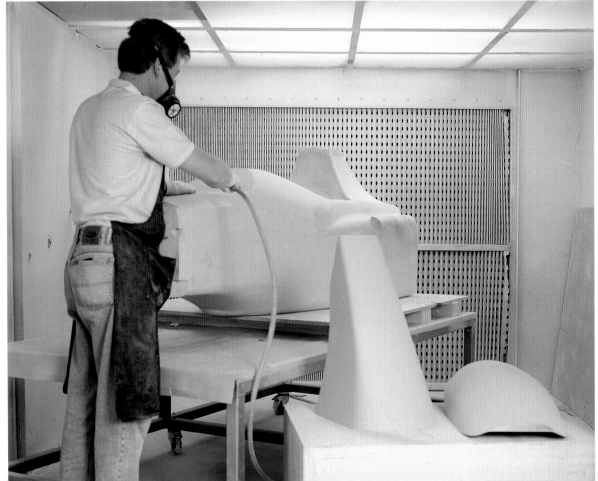

stabilize it – by releasing any volatile chemicals – then they are hand sanded with very fine (1000-grit) wet-or-dry paper.

At this stage, Lola Composites' Stiefelmayer three-axis digitizer – 'big brother' to the one in the model shop at Lola Cars – is used to verify that the finished patterns are faithful to the original CNC programs. In addition, the digitizer draws upon CAD data to plot the correct positions for holes that must be drilled in certain patterns. Some of these holes equate to the locations of certain inserts that must be positioned with exceptional accuracy, while others – slightly larger – equate to points where small, removable patterns known as tooling blocks will be fitted in the molds shortly before the panels are laid-up. Tooling blocks allow apertures and recesses to be formed in panels – for example, at the points where the foremost wishbone mounts are recessed into the front of the chassis, and where the aft legs of the front wishbones pass through the sides of the chassis.

Apertures and recesses are usually incorporated to improve the streamlining at points where wishbone mounts and other such protuberances would induce aerodynamic drag.

## Mold making

The process of producing molds from the eight chassis patterns is undertaken at Lola Composites' Clifton Road site. The molds are made from pre-preg carbon fiber incorporating an epoxy resin. This bestows thermal stability, ensuring that the molds don't expand and distort when they're exposed to the very high temperatures necessary to cure the chassis panels.

Before mold making can get under way, the patterns must be thoroughly prepared. To allow a ninety-degree angle to be introduced at the edges of the molds, thereby bestowing strength and rigidity, a melamine shelf is attached to the entire perimeter of the bottom edge of each pattern. These shelves are known as weirs, or returns, and are seldom less than 6in (150mm) wide. To ensure that the molds will separate cleanly, each pattern is given three coats of release agent (Frekote), then buffed to a high sheen with three coats of hard wax (Simoniz). A slate powder-based gel coat is applied and left to dry overnight.

As mentioned in the previous section, some of the patterns bear holes at points where inserts must be positioned with exceptional accuracy, and where tooling blocks are required. Although the tooling

*Each pattern receives a slate powder-based gel coat, which is left to dry overnight.*

blocks won't be installed until just before the laminators start laying-up the panels in the molds, and the inserts won't be fitted until an even later stage, the mold makers fit short steel and nylon dowels into each of the holes at this stage. Steel dowels are employed at points where the completed mold will slide cleanly off them, while nylon dowels are employed at points where it will not: the latter simply snap in two. The mold makers fix a drill bush onto each of the dowels that mark an insert location, and a threaded steel grommet onto each of the dowels that mark a tooling block location.

With these tasks completed, the mold making process can commence. The molds for some chassis panels are made in three pieces – a central section and two detachable ends – to aid removal of the completed panels, particularly in cases where they might otherwise become 'trapped.' Additional weirs are incorporated to delineate the divisions in such molds. A total of ten layers of carbon fiber of two different weights are laid-up atop each pattern to make a typical mold. To impart rigidity, the fibers of each layer are oriented at forty-five degrees to those of the layer below.

After the first two layers of the mold have been laid-up, steps are taken to compact them together and force them against the contours of the pattern. The pattern/mold combination is enveloped in a tailored vacuum bag and a vacuum state – typically, 26in of mercury – is induced, consolidating and debulking the layup. Great skill is required when tailoring the vacuum bag, as it must conform closely

*A total of ten layers of carbon fiber are laid-up atop each pattern to make a typical mold.*

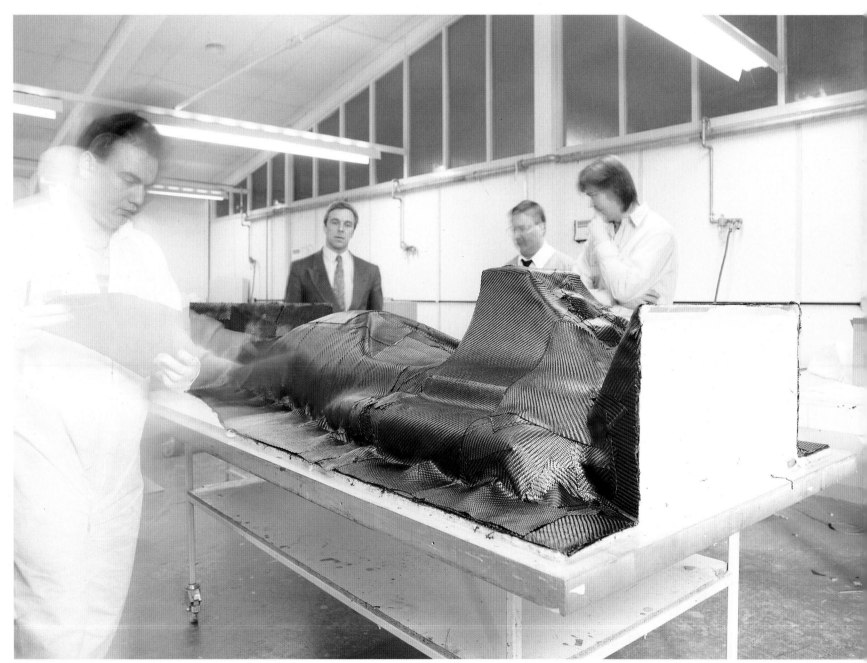

enough to ensure that the carbon fiber is pressed firmly into all the features of the mold when the air is drawn out, but the fit must not be so snug as to result in the bag being torn. Although the plastic is strong, and stretches, it can still be damaged.

A vacuum bag is applied again several times during the layup process. When the tenth and final layer is in place, however, an additional process is undertaken. A prolonged debulk, it increases the fiber-to-resin ratio considerably – bestowing greater strength. A layer of cotton wool-like polyester cloth known as a breather layer is sandwiched between the carbon fiber and the vacuum bag, then the pattern/mold combination is exposed to a state of vacuum for a period of one hour. By this process, excess resin is drawn from the carbon fiber, together with certain volatile chemicals. Both are deposited on the breather layer. A non-stick film known as a release layer, placed between the breather layer and the vacuum bag, ensures that the two don't stick together. After this process, the release layer is simply peeled off and discarded.

With this task completed, the pattern/mold combination is ovened for ten hours at a temperature of 45degC (113degF) to cure the mold. Additional reinforcement (known as 'eggboxing') is then built

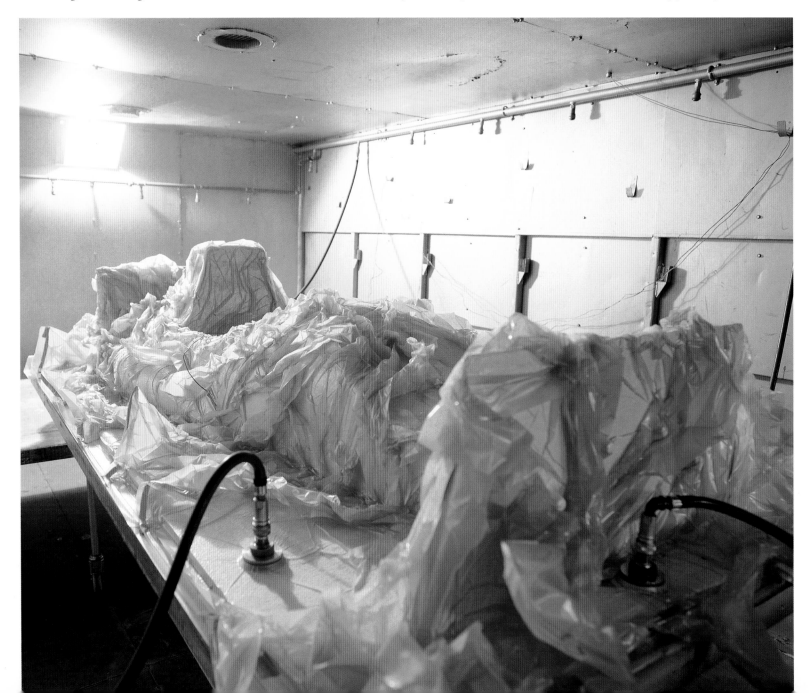

into the back of the mold, right up to the underside of the periphery weiring.

When the completed mold is lifted away from the pattern and weiring, it slides off the steel dowels, the nylon dowels break, but the drill bushes and threaded steel grommets – being integral with the mold – remain there to serve as fixings for dowels that will locate the inserts, and as points to which the tooling blocks can be bolted.

Soon after, the mold is returned to the oven and post-cured to 150degC (300degF) – some 20degC (70degF) above its normal operating temperature. This stabilizes the mold by removing any inherent stresses.

It only remains to prepare the molds for their first use. Each mold is degreased with a solvent (Acetone) to remove any contaminants, then receives no less than ten coats of release agent. Each coat is left to evaporate before the next application. If necessary, the mold is buffed after the fifth coat to maintain a high surface sheen. The mold is then placed in the oven and heated at a minimum temperature of 100degC (120degF) for 30-60 minutes. This hardens the release agent, baking it into the mold.

The second and subsequent uses of the mold require only a single coat of release agent.

*The completed mold for the lower half of the chassis. As can be seen here, molds for some chassis panels are made in three pieces – a central section and two detachable ends – to aid removal of the completed panels, particularly in cases where they might otherwise become 'trapped.'*

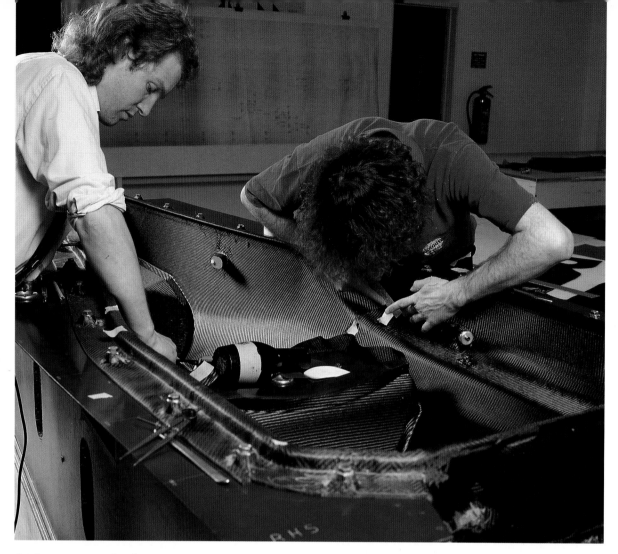

*Somewhat at variance with the high-tech nature of carbon fiber structures produced for Formula 1, the layup process is a labor-intensive activity involving almost wholly manual techniques.*

## Carbon-composite layup

Formula 1 chassis structures are composed of two multi-ply carbon fiber skins sandwiching a layer of aluminium honeycomb core material. The lower half of a chassis, for example, typically comprizes five layers of carbon fiber, a layer of aluminium honeycomb, and five more layers of carbon fiber.

The chassis panels for the Lola BMS-Ferrari T93/30 – in common with all Lola Cars' carbon-composite structures – were produced at Lola Composites' Clifton Road site. Consistent with Lola's traditional role of mass producing race cars, kits of carbon fiber pieces are produced to streamline the layup process. The chassis of the Lola BMS-Ferrari T93/30, being composed of eight panels, required eight different kits to be formulated, then produced in quantities that varied according to the envisaged attrition rates. Nose cones tend to be produced in the largest quantities!

Initially, a low cost prototype kit is assembled

for each panel, with pre-preg fiberglass being used in place of pre- preg carbon fiber. Lola's in-house composites engineer is closely involved in the assembly of the prototype kits, as it's essential that the layup of each panel fulfils his structural requirements. The manner in which carbon fiber 'flows' through compound curves tends to produce load distribution patterns more sophisticated than the computational predictions generated by the FEA system, so Tyler adopts a hands-on approach to ensure that reality matches theory.

Pre-preg fiberglass is far more suitable for the prototype kits than conventional dry mat fiberglass because it conforms to the contours of the molds in much the same manner as pre- preg carbon fiber. This quality, known as drapability, is vital to a successful layup.

One by one, the fiberglass pieces are laid into the appropriate mold and trimmed to the desired shape, but the resin is at no stage activated. When

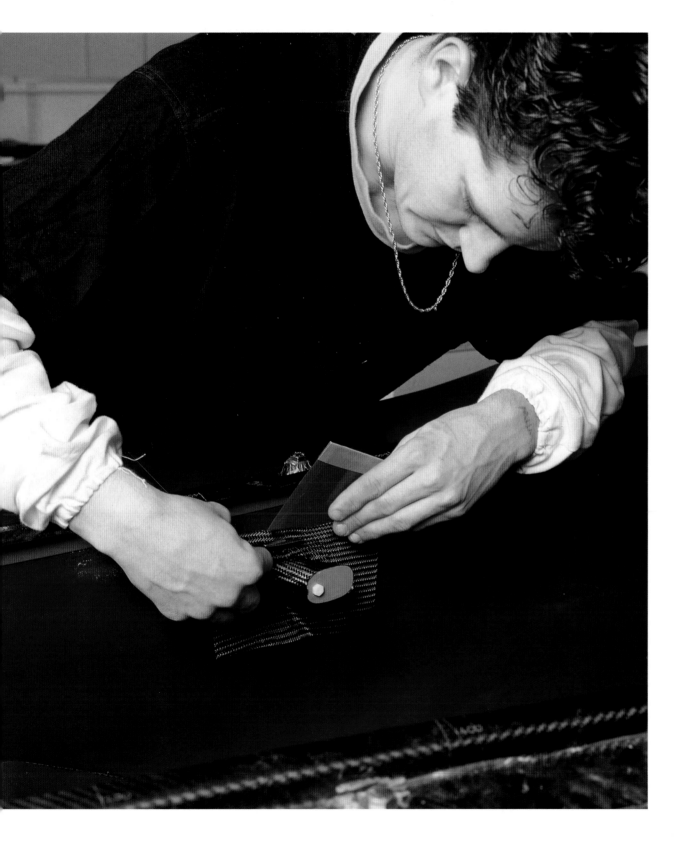

The carbon fiber pieces are slightly oversized, so that the laminators can trim them down to create the correct amount of overlap. They place a sheet of thick plastic behind the piece they're trimming as a safeguard against scoring the surface of the mold – as seen here, where the laminator is working the material around a tooling block.

The presence of resin within the fibers simplifies the task of laying-up the carbon fiber, as it makes the material slightly sticky at room temperature, preventing it from slipping from the sides of the mold after it's been pressed on. This quality is known as tack. Here, a laminator brushes a smear of resin onto the mold to augment the tack.

all of the pieces have been cut to size, they are removed from the mold and laid flat to serve as a basis for aluminium templates from which the carbon fiber pieces themselves will be cut.

Producing the prototype kit and cutting the templates for the chassis takes two to three days, because a substantial number of templates must be made and extensive documentation is required. This documentation provides a basis for explicit written and diagrammatical instructions issued to those who undertake the layup: the laminators. The intention is not to deskill their role, but to eliminate the need for interpretation, which would be time-consuming, and to lessen the possibility of errors. When the first panel is laid-up, the instructions are usually amended slightly to account for differences between what was considered theoretically suitable and what,

in reality, proved practical.

Each template is marked with a unique reference number keyed to information relating to the manner in which pieces of carbon fiber cut from it will be laid in the mold. In-house specialists then cut the kits, recording the appropriate raw material batch number as they go, so that the batch can be traced back to its original certificate of conformance in the unlikely event of quality-control concerns.

Before commencing the lay-up procedure, the laminators bolt the tooling blocks into the molds, and install nylon dowels at points where these are required to locate certain inserts. Tooling blocks are generally made from Tufnol or aluminium.

Somewhat at variance with the high-tech nature of carbon fiber structures produced for Formula 1, the layup process is a labor-intensive activity involv-

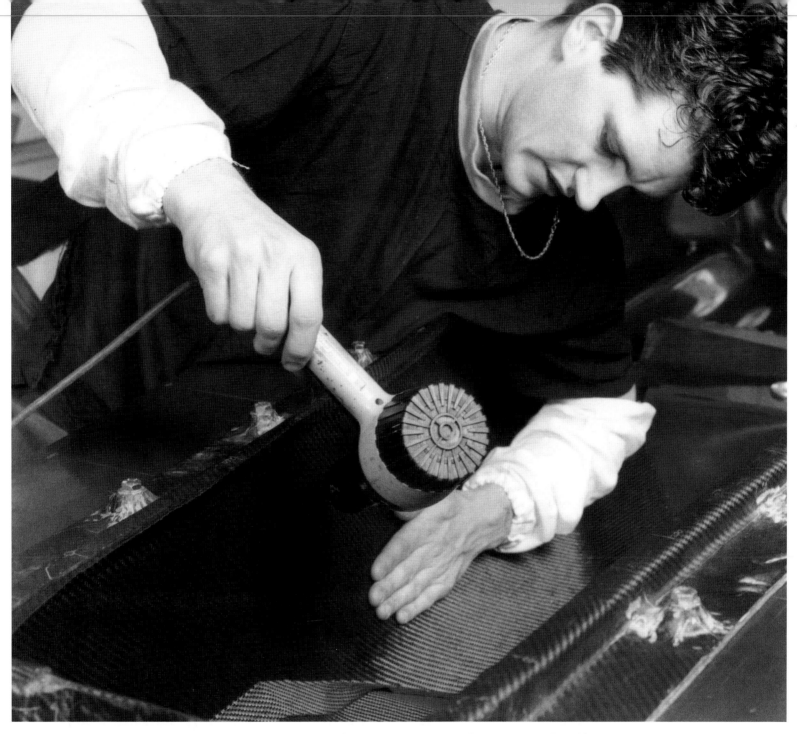

ing almost wholly manual techniques. The requisite skills can only be acquired through experience, and center on an intimate understanding of how materials are placed in molds, and how pieces overlap to form joints. At regular intervals throughout the lay-up procedure, quality control inspectors monitor activities to ensure that the proper standards are maintained.

The layup requirements for pre-preg carbon fiber differ from those of conventional dry mat fiberglass in several major respects. With dry mat fiberglass, the mold is treated with a gel coat, then one or more layers are placed in the mold and a mixture of resin and a catalyst is worked in with a brush and/or a metal roller to ensure that the mat is thoroughly saturated. The resin cures at room tem-

*The laminators warm the carbon fiber through with hair dryers to soften the resin, making the fabric more pliable and increasing the tack.*

*As well as hair dryers, laminators use surgical blades and spatulas to work the material into the contours of the mold and around the tooling blocks.*

perature, then the finished panel is eased from the mold.

With pre-preg carbon fiber there is no need for a gel coat, nor is there any need to apply resin, because resin is already impregnated into the fibers. Similarly, there is no need for a catalyst, as the resin is activated by the application of heat at a later stage. At high temperatures, the resin flows into the surrounding fibers, causing the carbon fiber to cure.

The presence of resin within the fibers simplifies the task of laying-up the carbon fiber, as it makes the material slightly sticky at room temperature, preventing it from slipping from the sides of the mold after it's been pressed on. This quality is known as tack. It is essential that the carbon fiber conforms to the contours of the mold and doesn't bridge any

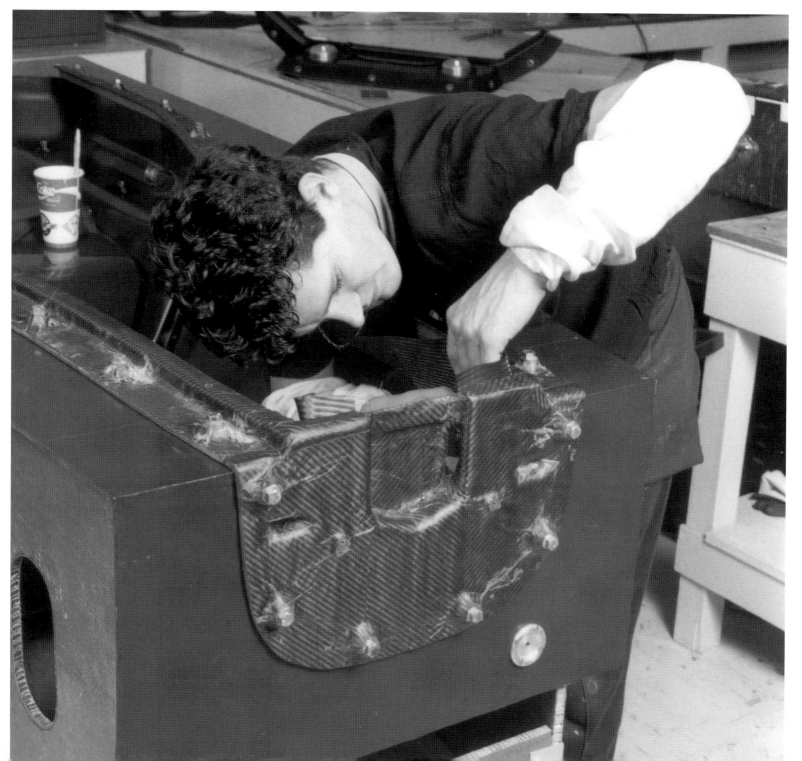

This photo shows how the carbon fiber pieces are applied in combinations of orientations that accord to the required structural properties of the panel. This is the upper half of the chassis: the triangular feature in the center is the cockpit opening.

Chassis panels are cured in an autoclave, where a combination of extreme heat and high pressure are applied atop the vacuum state. A typical heat level in the autoclave is 125degC (260degF), while the pressure level typically is 60-90psi, but can be as high as 100psi. As a precaution against fire, the autoclave at Lola Composites is charged with pressurized nitrogen, as opposed to pressurized air.

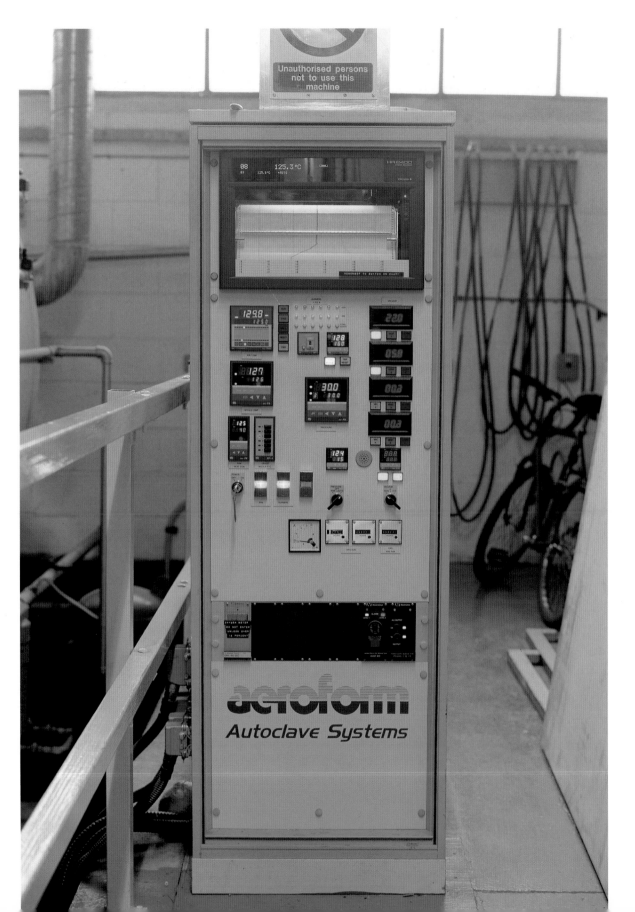

Close-up view of the
control and monitoring
console for Lola
Composites' autoclave.

*The multi-ply carbon fiber construction is only part of the total structure. The carbon fiber layers form two skins that sandwich an aluminium honeycomb core material to produce a structure of immense rigidity and strength – and, vitally, low weight. Here, pieces of aluminium core are being placed atop the outer skin.*

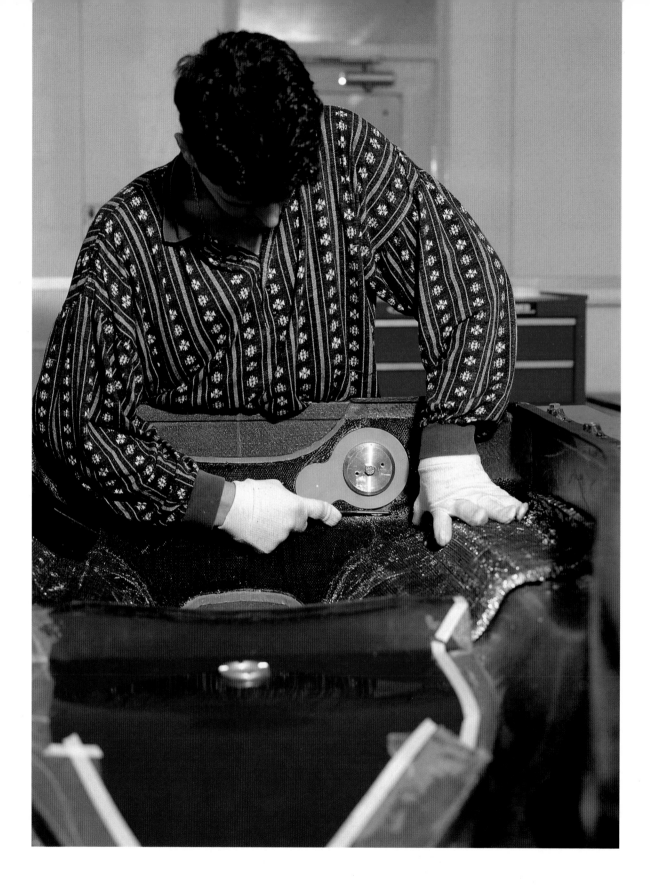

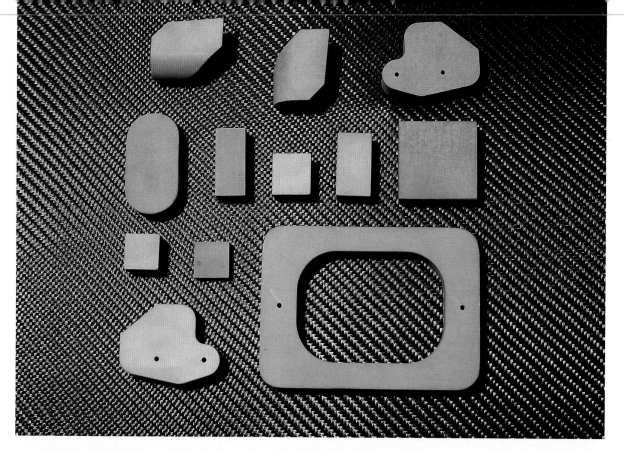

Local reinforcements – known as inserts – are incorporated to counter concentrated loads exerted where retention bolts for the front damper mounts and wishbone mounts, the sidepods, and other fittings will pass through the carbon-composite/aluminium honeycomb structure. The majority are made from a laminated polypropylene material tradenamed Tufnol, seen here.

The inserts are incorporated into the structure at the same time as the aluminium honeycomb core material.

of the corners or other features, so the laminators warm it through with hair dryers to soften the resin, making the fabric more pliable and increasing the tack. They can also brush a smear of resin onto the mold to augment the tack.

Paying meticulous attention to the composite engineer's instructions, the laminators apply the carbon fiber pieces in combinations of materials and orientations that accord to the required structural properties of the panel. As well as hair dryers, they use surgical blades and spatulas to work the material into the contours of the mold and around the tooling blocks, taking care to ensure that pockets of air aren't trapped between the plies. The carbon fiber pieces are slightly oversized, so that the laminators can trim them down to create the correct amount of overlap. They place a sheet of thick plastic behind the piece they're trimming as a safeguard against scoring the surface of the mold.

Chassis panels are composed of both woven carbon fiber fabrics and unidirectional (non-woven) carbon fiber tape. The woven fabrics range from heavy carbon weaves to light carbon weaves, with thicknesses varying from 10-15 thousandths of an inch, reducing to 8-13 thousandths of an inch when cured. The unidirectional tape typically is 6 thousandths of an inch thick and cures down to a thickness of 5 thousandths of an inch. Anyone viewing a finished carbon fiber structure without knowledge of how it went together could be forgiven for thinking that the overlapping joints are, in fact, butt joints. The carbon fiber is so thin, when cured, that the overlap is visually indistinguishable.

Although the carbon fiber is thin, it's extremely concentrated: that is to say, its fiber content is incredibly high. To achieve a cured thickness of just 1/32in (1mm) can involve building up three or four layers of material! In their uncured state, the materials aren't particularly compacted, even when they've been sealed in a vacuum bag and subjected to a high state of vacuum to ensure that they're forced firmly together, and are pressed tightly into the corners and other features of the mold. It is only later – when the mold/panel combination is placed in an autoclave for a combination of extreme heat and high pressure to be applied atop the vacuum state – that the materials become truly compacted.

Chassis panels are cured in an autoclave because – unlike the molds from which they're produced – they are load bearing structures. A typical heat level in the autoclave is 125degC (260degF), while the pressure level typically is 60-90psi, but can be as high as 100psi. As a precaution against fire, the autoclave at Lola Composites is charged with pressurized nitrogen, as opposed to pressurized air. The vacuum state typically is 26in of mercury. When the correct pressure level has been reached, the vacuum is dumped. Chassis panels are usually exposed to the combination of heat, pressure and the vacuum state for a period of two and a half hours.

A chassis panel 'visits' the autoclave three times: once, after the outer skin has been laid-up, again after the honeycomb core material and inserts have been incorporated, and again after the inner skin has been laid-up. When the mold/panel combination is removed from the autoclave following curing of the outer skin, it is left to cool down for an hour or so before the laminators begin placing the precut pieces of aluminium honeycomb core material on top of it. Great precision is required, because if the core does not adhere evenly to both skins, loads will be unevenly distributed. A sheet of neat resin applied between the core material and the outer carbon fiber skin creates an exceptionally strong bond when cured.

Generally speaking, the composites engineer will have attempted to keep the core material as thick as possible, but there are regions known as core relief positions where its thickness must be reduced. For example, there tends to be a region of thinner core material in the upper half of the chassis, immediately in front of the cockpit opening, to create the necessary clearance for the driver's hands on the steering wheel. Similarly, there is a region of thinner core material in the lower half of the chassis, where the foot pedal mounting plate will be situated. Core thicknesses vary from 1/4-3/4in (6-18mm).

The inserts are placed atop the outer carbon fiber skin at the same time as the aluminium core material. The majority are made from a laminated polypropylene material tradenamed Tufnol, while others are produced from carbon fiber or fashioned from solid aluminium. Inserts made from Tufnol and carbon fiber have thermal expansion properties that are 'in step' with the main carbon fiber structure, reducing the risk of distortion. Aluminium is less tolerant to thermally-induced expansion, so large aluminium inserts are avoided. Determining the sizes of the inserts is an important factor: they must be kept small to save weight, but they must be large enough to provide some leeway in the event of minor movement taking place during curing. Carbon fiber is employed when inserts are required on curved surfaces, as carbon fiber can be molded to virtually any shape.

None of the inserts are threaded until after the panel

has been removed from its mold – indeed, holes are rarely drilled in the inserts in advance: if they are, they're drilled to a smaller diameter than required and aren't drilled out to the proper size until the chassis is assembled. The reason for this is that, although the inserts are installed very precisely, they can displace slightly during the curing process.

When the aluminium honeycomb core material and the inserts are in place, the mold/panel combination is placed in a vacuum bag once more and wheeled back into the autoclave. This second curing bonds the honeycomb material and the inserts are bonded firmly to the outer carbon fiber skin.

After the mold/panel combination has been removed from the autoclave and the vacuum bag stripped off, the inner skin is laid-up atop the core. Again, a layer of neat resin is placed over the honeycomb material and inserts first, to ensure a firm bond. The carbon fiber pieces are laid-up in a 'mirror image' of the outer skin. When the final layer has been laid- up, the mold/panel combination is placed

in a vacuum bag yet again and wheeled into the autoclave for the last time. When it comes out, it's allowed to cool for about twenty minutes before the tooling blocks and nylon dowels are removed, at which point the panel is eased from its mold.

Each panel undergoes a series of detailed visual and dimensional inspections in the quality control department before it is delivered to Lola Cars for assembly. Indeed, the first few examples of each panel undergo non-destructive testing (NDT) at Lola Cars, to verify that they meet the required specification before approval is given to continue production. Lola Composites personnel take particular care to ensure that neighboring panels will fit together accurately. For example, the upper and lower chassis halves are connected by means of a tongue and groove joint, in which the upper half incorporates the tongue feature. The tongue and groove features are painstakingly trimmed to ensure that the overall depth of the chassis corresponds to the design drawings.

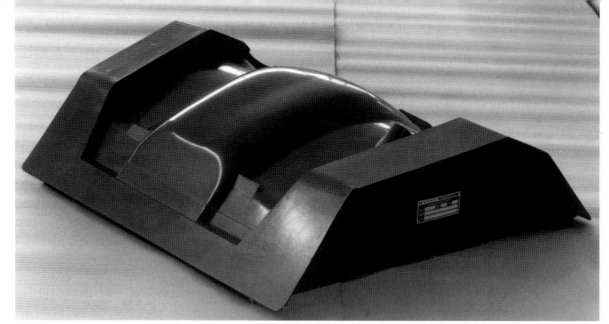

The mold for the Lola BMS-Ferrari T93/30's seat back structure.

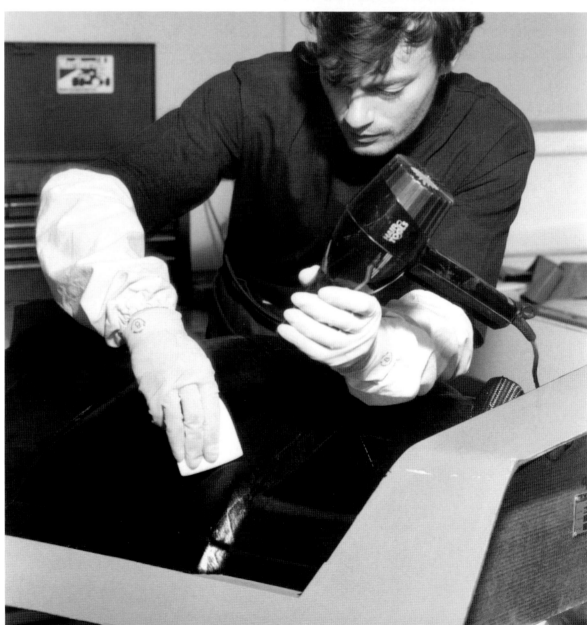

A laminator at work on the seat back, which is sculpted to accommodate the driver's torso.

## Assembly

When the chassis panels are completed, they leave Lola Composites' Clifton Road site for the chassis shop at Lola Cars' premises on Glebe Road. There, the chassis is assembled and outfitted.

Even while the layup process is in its final stages at Clifton Road, work gets under way at Glebe Road to prepare a jig upon which to assemble the chassis. This comprizes a rectangular-section horizontal steel beam bearing several adjustable platforms to which the chassis can be anchored squarely. The platforms also provide anchors for two flat steel templates that denote the precise locations in the front and rear walls of the chassis where holes must be drilled. These templates are cut from 1/4in (6mm) sheet steel, and the points where holes were required are identified from the design drawings and marked with extreme precision, then drilled out. The template for the front wall of the chassis denotes the points where holes are needed for items such as the mountings for the forward legs of the front suspension wishbones, the nose cone attachment fittings and the three master cylinders, while the template for the rear bulkhead denotes the points where holes are needed for such items as the upper engine mounts and the fire extinguishant delivery pipe.

Particular care must be taken when drilling holes to ensure that they are all in the same plane, or the completed car will not sit squarely on the ground. Likewise, accuracy in the positioning of drill holes is essential to ensure that interchangeable panels – nose cones and damper hatches – will, indeed, be readily interchangeable.

When all of the holes have been drilled, the templates are removed, whereupon certain holes can

*The upper half of the Lola BMS-Ferrari T93/30's chassis in the assembly shop at Lola Cars' Glebe Road premises.*

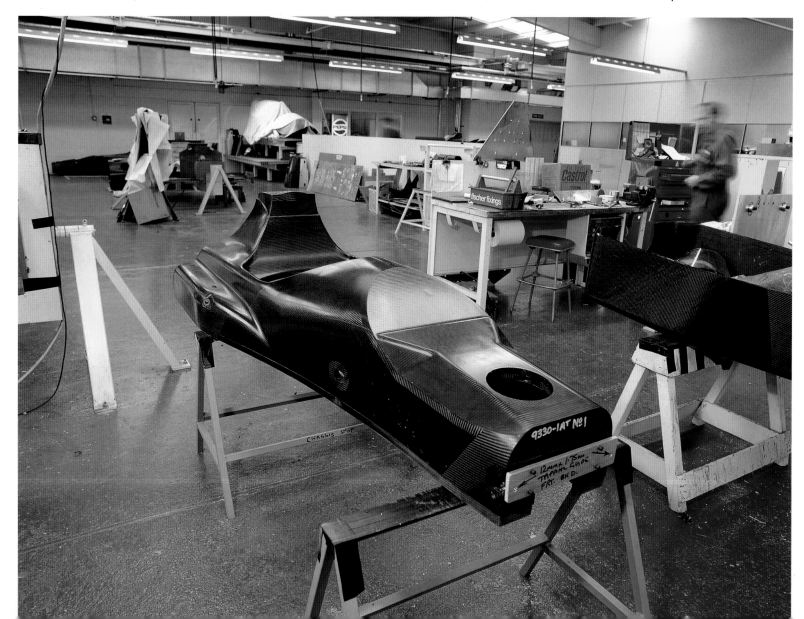

*A compound-curvature fiberglass template is employed to ensure accurate drilling of holes along the top of the chassis. The holes will facilitate fitment of such items as the damper mounts and other front suspension elements.*

be enlarged, tapped or countersunk as required.

Holes must be drilled in the underside of the lower chassis half to accommodate the bolts that retain the undertray and external fittings such as the lower engine mounts, as well as internal fittings such as the foot pedal mounting plate. A third flat steel template is produced for this purpose and affixed firmly to the upturned lower chassis half so that holes can be drilled straight through. Again, after the template is removed, certain holes are enlarged, tapped or countersunk as required.

In addition to the flat steel templates affixed to the underside of the chassis and to the front and rear bulkheads, three compound-curvature fiberglass templates are produced to facilitate accurate drilling of holes along the top and sides of the chassis. Molded from the relevant chassis patterns, they correspond to the region of the upper chassis that will lie beneath the damper hatch, and to the regions of the chassis flanks where the sidepods will be attached. Holes drilled through these three templates will facilitate fitment of such items as the damper mounts and other front suspension elements, and will allow the sidepods to be fitted at a later stage.

Many more holes are drilled in the chassis halves without the aid of templates. They facilitate the installation of various fittings in the cockpit, the fuel cell compartment and elsewhere at a later stage. By the time the chassis leaves for the final assembly area, virtually all of the required holes have been drilled. As a health precaution, carbon dust is drawn away through an ever-present length of vacuum cleaner hose.

Before the upper and lower chassis halves are mated permanently, the three bulkheads – the seat back, the dash bulkhead and the rocker bulkhead – are installed: also, in the case of the Lola BMS-Ferrari T93/30, the two engine mount bracing tubes. The three bulkheads are fixed to the upper chassis panel initially, and are only joined to the lower panel when the two chassis halves are mated. They are, however, all placed temporarily in the lower panel for scrupulous fit checks.

Sculpted to accommodate the driver's torso, the seat back is a carbon-composite/aluminium honeycomb sandwich structure that forms the boundary between the fuel cell compartment and the cockpit. Bonded and rivetted in, it contributes to the

*Holes must be drilled in the underside of the lower chassis half to accommodate the bolts that retain the undertray and external fittings such as the lower engine mounts, and internal fittings such as the foot pedal mounting plate. A flat steel template is affixed to the upturned lower chassis half.*

A template is affixed to the front wall of the chassis to denote the points where holes are needed for items such as the mountings for the forward legs of the front suspension wishbones, the nose cone attachment fittings, and the three master cylinders.

overall rigidity of the chassis by countering any tendency it might have to lozenge under cornering or impact loads, and triangulates the region where loads are fed into the chassis from the engine mount bracing tubes. It bears inserts at the points where local reinforcement is required for the seat belt mounts and the bellcrank that carries the gear shift linkage.

The dash bulkhead is fitted immediately forward of the cockpit opening. It serves as the mounting point for the aft legs of both front wishbones – for which it bears inserts – and has a large central aperture through which the driver's legs pass. It is a flat carbon-composite/aluminium honeycomb sandwich structure about 1in (25mm) thick, with a substantial flange around much of its perimeter. This

*Installing the anodized aluminium foot pedal mounting plate in the lower half of the chassis.*

The dash bulkhead is a flat carbon-composite/aluminium honeycomb sandwich structure that's fitted immediately forward of the cockpit opening. It serves as the mounting point for the aft legs of both front wishbones, and has a large central aperture through which the driver's legs pass.

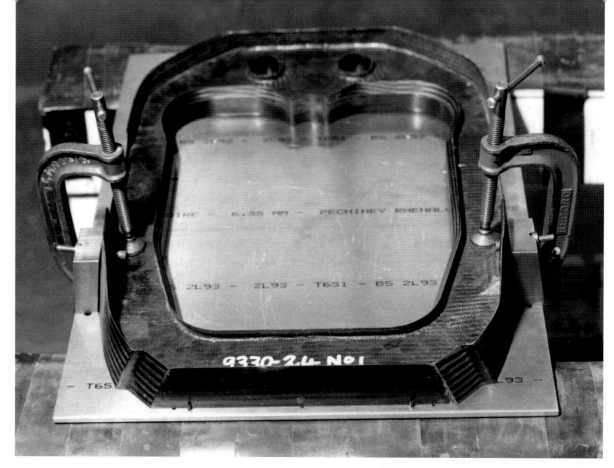

A flat steel template is produced to denote the locations of holes that must be drilled in the dash bulkhead, to carry the mounting points for the steering column and the dashpanel, and allow the throttle cable to pass through.

Conducting fit checks between the dash bulkhead and the inverted upper half of the chassis. When bonded and rivetted in, it will contribute to the rigidity of the chassis by countering any tendency it might have to lozenge under cornering or impact loads. Also visible from this angle – in the footwell, roughly half way between the dash bulkhead and the front wall of the chassis – is the rocker bulkhead: a horseshoe shaped anodized aluminium structure that reinforces the chassis in the region where loads are fed in from the front pushrods, and also contributes to the overall rigidity of the chassis.

*The seat back is a carbon-composite/aluminium honeycomb sandwich structure that forms the boundary between the fuel cell compartment and the cockpit. Note the two recesses at the top that will accommodate the driver's shoulder straps, and the recess on the right side for the bellcrank that will carry the gear shift linkage.*

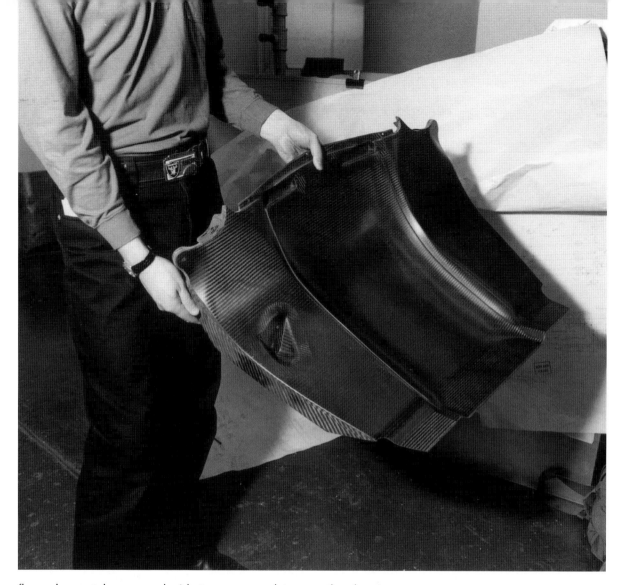

flange has notches on each side to accommodate the wishbone legs. Like the seat back, the dash bulkhead is bonded and rivetted in, and contributes to the rigidity of the chassis by countering lozenging. It also carries the mounting points for the steering column and the dashpanel.

A flat steel template is produced to denote the locations of holes that must be drilled in the dash bulkhead – allowing the throttle cable to pass through, and so on. These holes are drilled before the dash bulkhead is fixed to the upper half of the chassis.

In the footwell, roughly half way between the dash bulkhead and the front of the chassis, the rocker bulkhead is installed. It is a horseshoe shaped anodized aluminium structure about 1.5in (35mm) thick that reinforces the chassis in the region where loads are fed in from the front pushrods. Bolted and bonded in, it also contributes to the overall rigidity of

the chassis.

The Lola BMS-Ferrari T93/30's engine mount bracing tubes were 1.5in (35mm) in diameter, were made from filament-wound carbon fiber, and had threaded titanium fittings bonded into each end. They were retained to the circular anodized aluminium load spreaders that constituted the upper engine mounts, extended forwards through two tunnels in the fuel cell, and bolted to fittings bonded into the chassis walls either side of the seat back. To facilitate removal of the fuel cell, the fittings at either end of the tubes could be undone, allowing the tubes to be pulled out backwards through the 2in (50mm) diameter holes in the interlocking outer and inner elements of the engine mounts.

Any evidence of the engine mount bracing tubes was obscured when the engine and sidepods were in place, so they were undetectable to all but the

Undertaking fit checks between the seat back and the inverted upper half of the chassis. When bonded and rivetted in, it will contribute to the overall rigidity of the chassis by countering any lozenging tendencies, and will triangulate the region where loads are fed into the chassis from the engine mount bracing tubes.

Close-up view of the bonded and rivetted joint between the seat back and the inverted upper half of the chassis.

Perhaps uniquely, two removable carbon fiber bracing tubes were installed in the Lola BMS-Ferrari T93/30 to help disperse the fore and aft loads fed into the chassis from the upper engine mounts. They were an ingenious response to the structural challenges posed by the fact that some Formula 1 engines are narrower than the chassis to which they are fitted.

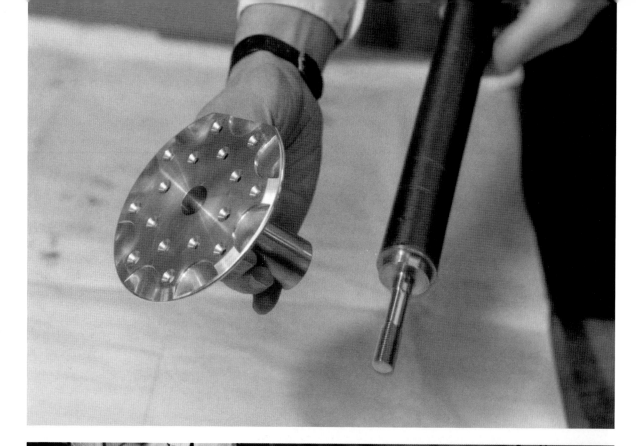

The engine mount bracing tubes had threaded titanium fittings bonded into each end. The tubes were retained to the circular anodized aluminium load spreaders that constituted the upper engine mounts, extended forwards through two tunnels in the fuel cell, and bolted to fittings bonded into the chassis walls either side of the seat back.

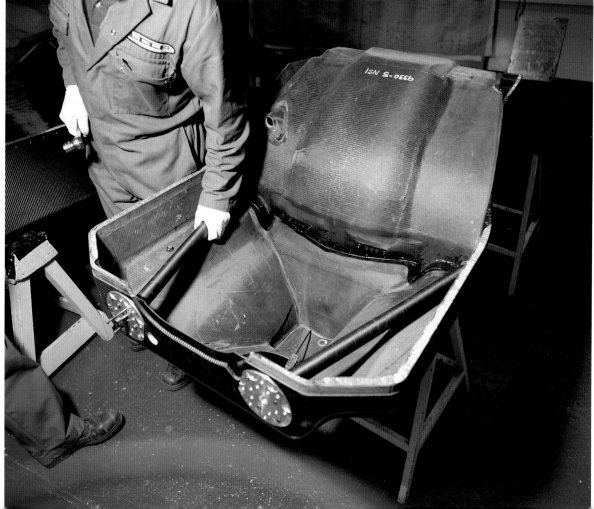

When all of the internal reinforcing elements were installed, a liberal application of epoxy adhesive was brushed onto the tongue and groove features of the upper and lower chassis halves respectively, then the upper half was eased down and rivets were inserted into a line of drill holes along the entire length of the upper-to-lower chassis interface.

most astute observer. Bracing tubes were probably unique to the Lola BMS-Ferrari T93/30, but this was impossible to verify with certainty at the time of writing, as teams tend to be tight lipped about such matters. They were Eric Broadley's ingenious response to the structural challenges posed by the fact that some Formula 1 engines are narrower than the chassis to which they are fitted. Engines have evolved to a narrower format – indeed, become smaller overall – as part of efforts to improve the flow of air over the engine cover to the rear aerofoil ensemble; also to reduce engine weight. Generally speaking, chassis have become wider in order to accommodate fuel in a manner that's conducive to reducing the wheelbase: part of efforts to improve weight distribution by placing a greater proportion of the car's weight on the front tires. In this particular case, the problem was exacerbated by the high fuel consumption of the Ferrari engine. While cars powered by the Ford-Cosworth HB require a fuel capacity of only 51.5USgal (195ltr), the chassis of the Lola BMS-Ferrari T93/30 had to accom-

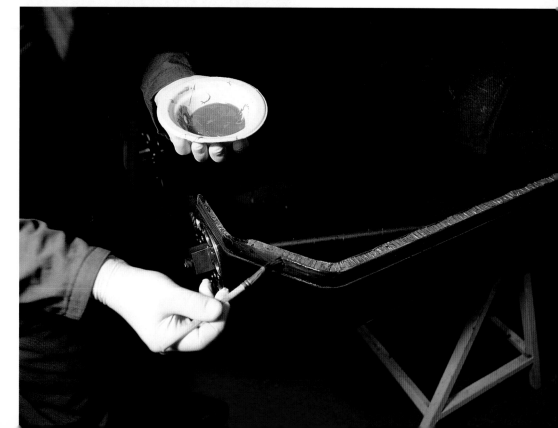

After the customary fit checks, the rollover hoop was bonded into place then secured with titanium bolts. On the Lola BMS-Ferrari T93/30, this operation was complicated by the fact that the fire extinguisher activation ring was to be situated at the interface between the rollover hoop and the chassis.

*An early stage in the installation of the front suspension, with the rocker posts and the antiroll mechanism in situ.*

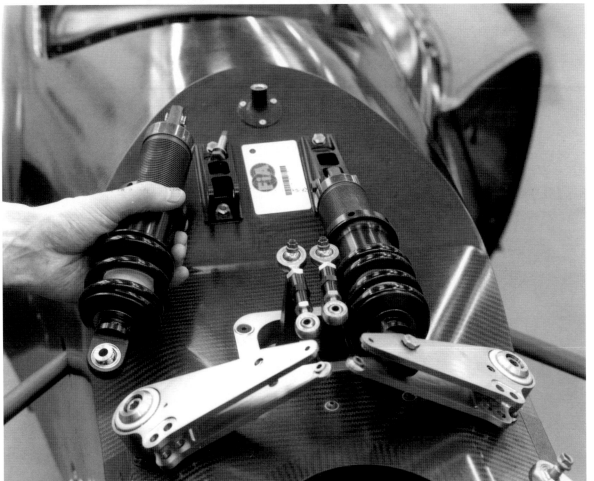

*Installation of the rockers and Koni dampers. The pushrods have yet to be attached to the rockers: they are merely resting on the chassis.*

modate a 60.7USgal (230ltr) fuel cell. While this volume of fuel could have been accommodated simply by making the car slightly longer, that would have increased the wheelbase to an unacceptable extent. Besides, the fuel cell width is limited by FISA regulations.

Purely from a structural standpoint, it would have been possible to disperse the fore and aft loads fed into the chassis from the engine by extending tubes *rearwards* and attaching them to a gearbox-mounted bulkhead, creating a semi-monocoque construction. This method of construction is employed on many race cars in which the engine is treated as a non-stress bearing member, including Formula 3 and Group C cars. On the grounds of practicality, however, this solution was deemed unaccept-

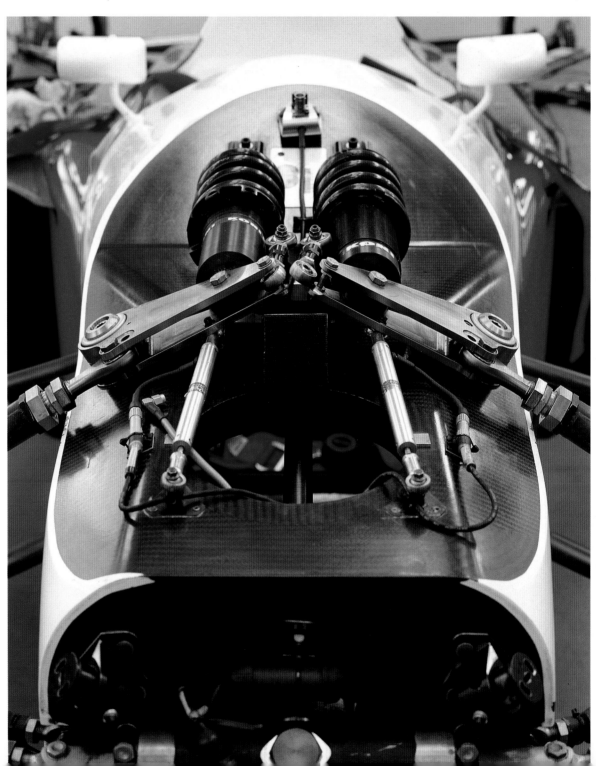

able. Having two fixed tubes over the top of the engine would limit accessibility, and the tubes could also be vulnerable to accident damage. It was a far more elegant solution to install them within the chassis, where they became 'fit and forget' items.

For all that, engine mount bracing tubes were an unwelcome addition to the Lola BMS-Ferrari T93/30, as they represented another weight penalty in an already weighty engine package.

When all five internal reinforcing elements – the three bulkheads and the two engine mount bracing tubes – were installed, a liberal application of 3M Scotchweld epoxy adhesive was brushed onto the tongue and groove features of the upper and lower chassis halves respectively, then the upper half was eased down and a line of drill holes and riv-

*A length of steel tape is taking the place of the left pushrod at this stage, but the upper and lower wishbones are already attached to their mountings.*

An overall view of the front of the Lola BMS-Ferrari T93/30, showing the inboard and outboard suspension elements, the steering rack and master cylinders (in plastic covers), and the (circular) transmitter for the on-board telemetry system.

The damper hatch in position.

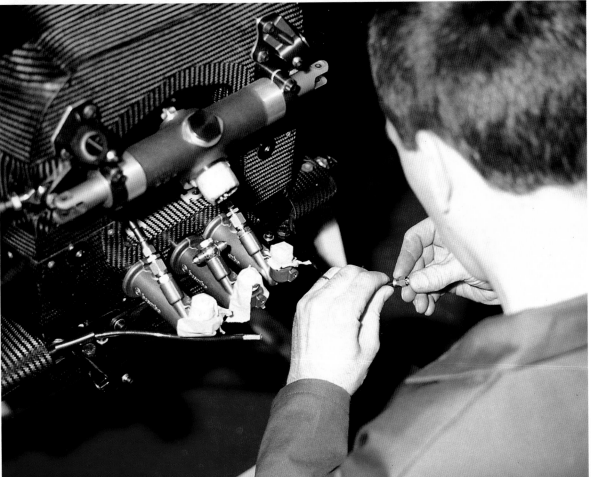

Installing plumbing for the braking system.

*Close-up views, from either side, of the Lola BMS-Ferrari T93/30's front brake installation.*

*The elements that constituted a front 'corner' on the Lola BMS-Ferrari T93/30. The uprights were fabricated by an outside (British) contractor.*

*A Brembo brake unit on the car's right front 'corner.' The brake pads were supplied by the French company Carbone Industrie*

*This 'exploded' view illustrates just how many parts go together to make a front upright. The template employed when fabricating the upright's central structure is shown in the background.*

ets were inserted along the entire length of the upper-to-lower chassis interface. Aluminium rivets with steel cores are employed for this purpose: 1/8in (3mm) rivets supplied by Avdel.

At this stage, after the customary fit checks, the rollover hoop was bonded into place then secured with titanium bolts. On the Lola BMS-Ferrari T93/30, this operation was complicated by the fact that the fire extinguisher activation ring was to be situated at the interface between the rollover hoop and the chassis. To facilitate fitment of the extinguisher activation mechanism at a later stage, two holes were drilled through the right wall of the chassis crown, a bracket installed behind it, and a slot cut at a corresponding point in the right side of the rollover hoop flange.

With the chassis structure complete, the cockpit was outfitted and the braking system was installed – as was the pushrod-activated front suspension. The uprights were fabricated by an outside (British) contractor, the brake units were manufactured by the Italian company Brembo, and the brake pads were supplied by the French company Carbone Industrie. The steering rack was connected to the front uprights by tubular steel trackrods with spherical bearings supplied by the British company NMB. Koni supplied the dampers, Goodyear provided the tires, and one of the companies in the Lucchini group – Due Emme Mille Miglia – supplied the wheel rims.

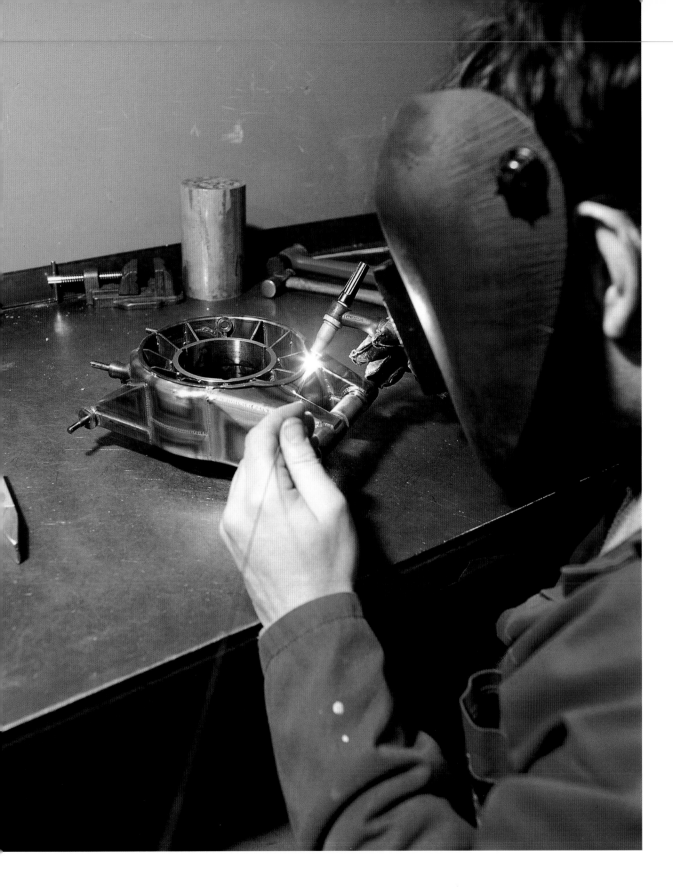

*Fabrication of a front upright.*

The Lola BMS-Ferrari T93/30's carbon fiber brake cooling ducts were manufactured in-house by Lola Composites. The front ducts comprized two elements, shown here.

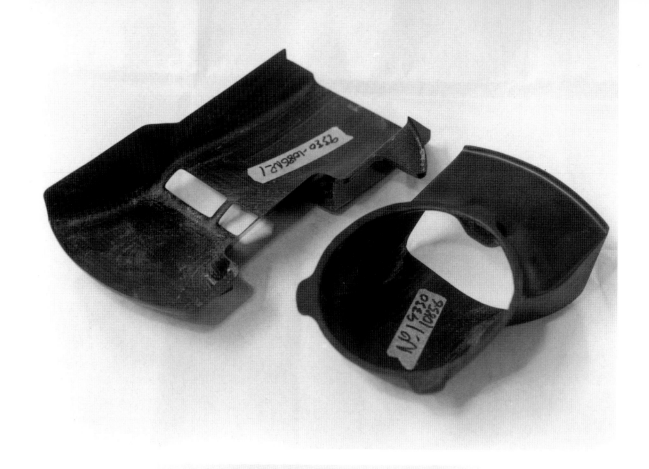

A fully assembled front brake duct.

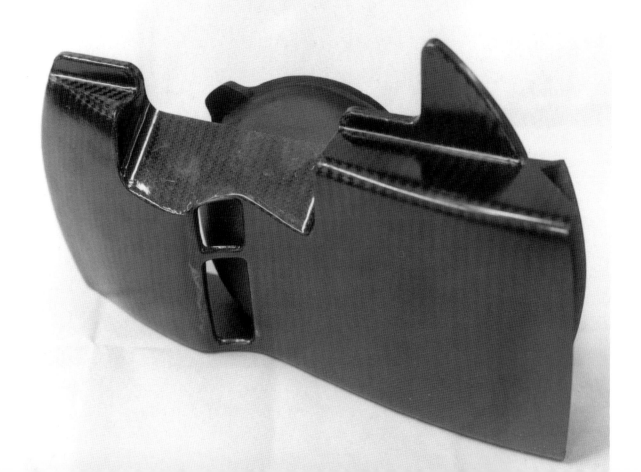

*A front wheel/tire assembly from the Lola BMS-Ferrari T93/30. One of the companies in the Lucchini group – Due Emme Mille Miglia – supplied the wheel rims. Goodyear provided the tires: the company is currently the sole supplier of tires in Formula 1.*

*Close-up view of the upright/brake assembly within the right front wheel rim, illustrating the economy of space.*

# CHAPTER 7

# Crash testing

**Mean deceleration values must not exceed twenty-five times the force of gravity for this aspect of the test to be deemed successful.**

To ensure that every Formula 1 car on the grid is capable of protecting its occupant in the event of an accident, FISA stipulates that each one of them must undergo a rigorous crash-testing program. The tests have been evolved over a long period of time, and are designed to simulate actual crash scenarios, safeguarding against the types of injuries typically inflicted on race-car drivers in the past.

A total of seven crash scenarios are simulated. They can be categorized under five headings, and are detailed below. The Lola BMS-Ferrari team has its crash testing undertaken at the Cranfield Impact Center, or CIC. Coincidentally, this is part of the Cranfield Institute of Technology, where Lola BMS-Ferrari conducts all its windtunnel testing.

Several other Formula 1 teams have their crash tests conducted at CIC: notably Benetton, Footwork, Lotus and Williams. Tests are also undertaken on roadgoing cars – for Ford, Rover and Volvo, among others. However, the Formula 1 tests are the most demanding.

**Head-on collision:** The first, and undoubtedly most spectacular, test simulates a head-on collision. It is designed to assess two things: the ability of the nose cone to protect the driver's feet and ankles from serious injury; and the ability of the chassis structure in general, and the nose cone in particular, to dissipate the kinetic energy released at the moment of impact, so that the driver is saved from injurious deceleration forces.

Such forces can cause internal organs such as the heart to be displaced, interrupting the blood supply with potentially fatal consequences. They can even, in extreme circumstances, cause the brain to become partially detached from the skull. This injury was sustained by Stirling Moss in 1962, in the accident that ended his career as a top-flight race driver.

Mean deceleration values must not exceed twenty-five times the force of gravity for this aspect of the test to be deemed successful.

The frontal crash test involves propelling the chassis structure down a ramp inclined at an angle of eleven degrees, to impact a thick steel plate supported in concrete. Deformation of the nose cone may extend back to the chassis structure, but must not reach the zone occupied by the driver's feet. This varies, depending on the design of the car, but is usually some 6in (150mm) aft of the nose cone/chassis interface. In fact, race car designers try to ensure that damage does not extend beyond the interface, as it's much simpler to replace a nose cone than it is to repair a chassis.

FISA regulations stipulate a minimum impact speed of 36.1fps (11mps) – equivalent to 24.75mph (39.82kph). This may seem unrepresentative of a real collision, but one must bear in mind that the steel plate yields *not an inch*, whereas a length of race-track guardrail protected by dozens of tires yields considerably.

Also, by the time a car strikes a tire wall, it's likely that much of its momentum will have been impeded by a sand trap.

To assess the effects on the car's occupant, and thus verify the ability of the chassis/nose cone structure to attenuate frontal impact forces, an instrumented anthropomorphic mannequin rides in the cockpit, strapped firmly in by a six- point racing safety harness.

FISA regulations specify that the chassis that undergoes the crash test must, assuming it passes the test, go on to actually race! Subsequent chassis of the same design need not undergo this particular test, but the team must prove to FISA's satisfaction that they are structurally identical. In order to increase the correlation of the frontal impact test to a real accident, the chassis under evaluation must bear the same loadings it will in race trim. A fuel cell is therefore mounted in the chassis – filled with water to simulate the mass of the real tank at the start of a race, and reproducing the structural loadings it generates at the moment of impact. For the same reason, a loaded fire extinguisher is mounted in the cockpit.

The chassis is then attached to a sturdy tubular-steel sled. It is joined at the engine mounting points, but merely supported underneath, not fixed down. The sled weighs 900lb (408kg) – representing the mass of the whole of the car aft of the chassis structure: the engine, gearbox, drivetrain, rear suspension units, and aerofoil ensembles. FISA regulations state that the sled/chassis combination, complete with mannequin and water-filled fuel cell, must weigh at least 1,720lb (780kg), so ballast is added when necessary.

Being joined only at the engine mounts, the sled's dynamics at the moment of impact accurately simulate the loadings transmitted into the rear of the chassis structure. Although a strap is tightened down over the cockpit to help secure the car on the sled, it is elastic enough to allow some vertical movement during the impact sequence.

The sled is suspended fractionally above the ramp on four air bearings, rather than running upon it on wheels – thereby removing rolling resistance as a potentially distorting influence on the test results. A degree of lateral guidance is, however, required, and a certain amount of rolling resistance is there-

*The chassis/sled combination prior to the head-on collision test. The nose cone is in another part of the building, being measured by a FISA official.*

fore induced. Roller bearings mounted on booms that extend sideways from the four corners of the sled, run parallel with rails on either side of the ramp. If the sled deviates by more than 1/2in (12mm) from its course, one or more of the roller bearings will momentarily make contact with the rails.

An electric hoist drives a length of chain that pulls the sled up the ramp. It is held by steel jaws for a short time at a predetermined spot near the top, while final instrumentation checks are completed, and all but one operative is either evacuated to a bunker area, or cleared to a safe distance. The lone operative then removes a safety bolt and retires to a safe distance, at which point the jaws are released by means of an air-driven plunger.

The sled is propelled down the ramp by a combination of two groupings of three bungee cords, assisted by gravity. The material from which the bungees are made is chosen for its progressive contraction properties – to ensure that the sled accelerates smoothly – and the elasticity of the bungees are carefully matched.

*Final preparations. With the nose cone attached, the chassis is ready for the test.*

The ramp is a cross-braced welded steel structure, with a deck of high-grade plywood covered with a layer of linoleum. CIC personnel polish the linoleum before each test to provide a uniformly smooth surface for the sled's air bearings to run over.

At the point of impact, a report akin to a rifle shot resounds around the walls of the test building. If all has gone according to plan, the nose cone should have collapsed progressively, absorbing the energy of the impact. The 1 in (25mm) sheet of steel bears visible evidence of the impact, but nei-ther buckles nor cracks. The sheet and its supporting structure are, in the parlance of the structural engineer, infinitely inflexible by comparison to the race car.

Instruments mounted on the aft end of the sled gather data on each run. Data are gathered at a very high rate, there being just 412 milliseconds of recording time, of which the impact itself occupies approximately 100 milliseconds. Two accelerometers measure the deceleration of the sled, from which the impact forces can be calculated. Data from either

*Photographic calibration lines are applied to the nose cone.*

is sufficient to support the test, for each acts as a backup to the other should one fail at the moment of impact. Two photoelectric cells on the left side of the sled, acting in concert with a beam of light projected from a fixed point on the ramp, allow the speed of the sled to be accurately measured. The data-gathering sequence is triggered when the beam of light activates the first cell.

The streams of data are relayed from the sled to a nearby control panel, via wires clustered together in protective rubber hoses suspended from the ceiling. Information can be viewed on monitors and reproduced in graph form at will.

At the crash test the author witnessed whilst researching this book, FISA technical delegates Charlie Whiting and Tom Kean were present to monitor proceedings and photograph key items of hardware: in particular, the nose cone before and after the crash test. The test itself was supervised by CIC's Dick Jones.

The whole event is recorded by a high-speed camera, and the sled is dotted with calibration markings to assist subsequent analysis of the impact sequence by the team. CIC contracts with the Kodak company to supply and operate the camera system. This records images digitally, as opposed to utilizing conventional film. Immediately after the test, a single videotape is produced for the car manu-

*Two key individuals prepare to monitor the head-on collision test from a console adjacent to the ramp. Dick Jones of Cranfield Impact Center (right) supervised the tests, while FISA technical delegate Tom Kean (left) was scrutinizing proceedings on behalf of motorsport's international governing body.*

facturer's use, then the camera system is powered down – irretrievably deleting all of the imagery.

Race-car manufacturers prefer this method of recording the impact to any other, as it is by far the most secure means of protecting technologically sensitive material.

**Nose cone side impact:** The second crash test simulates an accident in which the nose cone is struck heavily from the side. The intention is to verify that the nose cone will not become detached from the chassis under such circumstances, denuding the car of its most vital energy-absorbing structure. This test is therefore known as the 'nose push-off.'

The front aerofoils are strong enough to act as levers in this type of accident, wrenching the nose cone off.

Unlike the frontal impact simulation described earlier, this and the remaining tests are static, as opposed to dynamic, simulations. Every single chassis destined for Formula 1 races must undergo this test.

In preparation for the 'nose push-off test,' the chassis is anchored (at the engine mounting points only) to a sturdy tubular-steel framework. An oblong steel pad, measuring 12 x 4in (30 x 10cm), is positioned so as to contact the right side of the forward chassis structure, as close as possible to the interface with the nose cone, to brace the chassis firmly against the substantial loadings that are about to be exerted from the opposite side.

A second pad of identical dimensions is then positioned on the left side of the nose cone, 16in (40cm) forward of the front axle line. Unlike the other pad, which is fixed in position, this pad can translate slowly in a lateral direction by means of a worm-drive mechanism, exerting loadings equivalent to a major sideways impact.

*The chassis at the top of the eleven-degree ramp, bungee cords stretched tightly, seconds from the moment of release. The stepped nose arrangement, fashionable in Formula 1 over recent years, is seen particularly clearly from this angle. Note the two groupings of three bungee cords, and the markings for photographic calibration.*

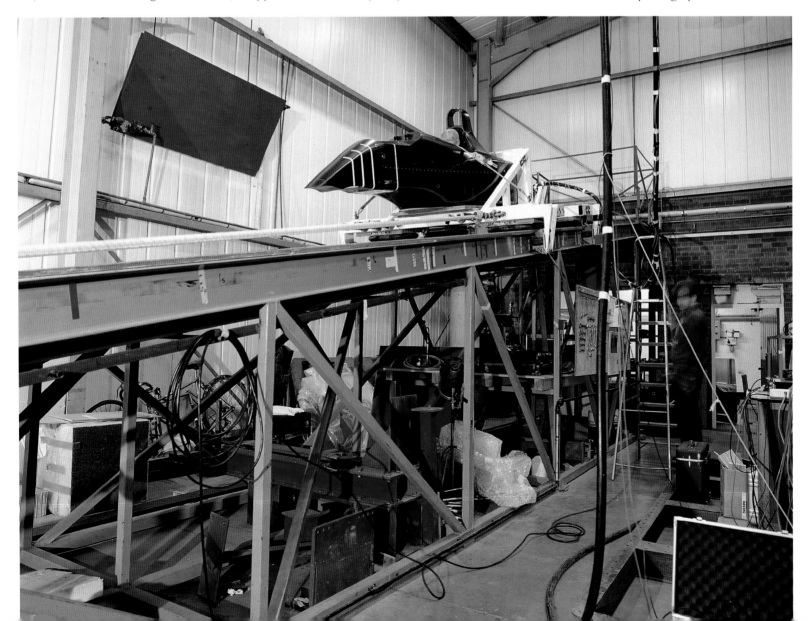

The worm-driven pad is equipped with a load cell to measure the lateral forces exerted on the chassis. It is activated until a force of 3 tons (30kN) has been exerted and held for a period of thirty seconds, and is then eased slowly away.

If this cycle is performed without any evidence of a structural failure, the FISA officials in attendance deem that the chassis has passed the 'nose push-off' test.

The instrumentation for the 'nose push-off' test comprises an electrical output from the load cell to a nearby computer/monitor, from which a graph is produced in real time. If the instrumentation detects that an increase in distortion is occurring independent of a corresponding increase in load (in which case the upward-curving line on the graph descends suddenly, indicating that a catastrophic failure has taken place, or is about to), the test may be abort-

*Nose cone of the Lola BMS-Ferrari T93/30 at the successful conclusion of the head-on collision test. Note that the nose cone structure has deformed progressively. The scroll of carbon fiber on the left of this picture is part of the top of the nose cone, which has curled harmlessly inwards, dissipating energy.*

ed on the instructions of the team, to preserve the structure for reinforcement.

**Chassis side impacts:** Three different – though comparable – crash scenarios are simulated with a sequence of 'squeeze tests,' in which the same pads employed for the 'nose push-off' test are used to compress the chassis structure laterally, simulating impacts from the side. Again, every single chassis destined for Formula 1 races must undergo this test.

For these tests, the chassis is braced at the back to prevent any longitudinal movement – otherwise, it might pop out from between the pads, as chassis of certain shapes are inclined to do – but it is free to move laterally. Measurements of displacement are made from *inside* the chassis, which is only deemed to have passed each of the three tests if it withstands a compression force of 2.5 tons (25kN) and springs back to within 0.04in (1mm) of its original shape, indicating that permanent distortion has not occurred. FISA regulations state that deformation must not exceed 3/4in (20mm), but this value is seldom – if ever – recorded, as structural failure would almost certainly have already occurred.

Subsequent chassis need only withstand a compression force of 2 tons (20kN) to pass the tests.

The first of these tests is designed to assess the ability of the chassis structure to resist front wheel/suspension unit intrusion into the footwell area. It is necessary to ensure that the front of the car will not collapse inwards, crushing the driver's feet and ankles.

An identical 'squeeze test' is conducted on the middle of the chassis, to assess the ability of the structure to resist a lateral intrusion into the region of the cockpit occupied by the driver's torso.

The third and final 'squeeze test' is conducted at the rear of the chassis, to assess the ability of the structure to resist a lateral intrusion into the fuel cell compartment, which might puncture the cell itself.

**Underside impact:** This test is similar to the lateral 'squeeze tests' described above, except that the chassis is placed on its side and only one pad – a circular pad 8in (20cm) in diameter – is applied to the underside, at a point immediately beneath the fuel cell compartment. In this respect, it can be regarded as a 'push test,' rather than a 'squeeze test.'

The intention is to assess the ability of the structure to resist intrusion into the underside of the fuel cell in the event of a major impact. To pass the test, the first chassis must withstand a compression force of 1.25 tons (12.5kN), while subsequent chas-

To assess the ability of the chassis to resist side impacts, a series of three 'squeeze tests' are undertaken. The chassis is braced at the back to prevent any longitudinal movement, but is free to move laterally. Pictured is the second of the tests, designed to ensure that the chassis can resist a lateral intrusion into the region of the cockpit occupied by the driver's torso.

To simulate an underside impact, the chassis is placed on its side and a load is applied to the region immediately beneath the fuel cell compartment.

sis need only withstand 1 ton (10kN).

Every single chassis destined for Formula 1 races must undergo this test.

**Rollover impact:** Only the first chassis destined for Formula 1 races must undergo this test.

A steel pad equipped with a load cell is slowly driven downwards onto the top of the rollover hoop by means of an hydraulic ram. The chassis is fixed to a tubular-steel platform inclined at a compound angle, in order to simulate a combination of loadings that equate to a rollover accident. Specifically, these loadings would comprise: a lateral component, as the car rolls over; a longitudinal component – exerted either forwards or backwards, depending on the car's orientation – imparted by the car's forward momentum; and a vertical component, as the car translates downwards onto the rollover hoop.

A load of 7.2 tons (72kN) is applied. The chassis

*With the chassis fixed at a compound angle, an hydraulic ram exerts a load of 7.2 tons (75kN) to the top of the rollover hoop. This simulates a combination of loadings that equate to a rollover accident.*

can be heard to creak and groan in the process. Nevertheless, the Lola BMS-Ferrari T93/30 passed the test without a hitch.

The gigantic rig CIC employs for this test is housed in Cranfield Institute of Technology's adjacent College of Aeronautics, and is capable of exerting vertical loadings as high as 150 tons (1500kN). Phenomenal loadings such as these typically are applied 'end-on' to lengths of carbon fiber tubing – not to race-cars!

When a chassis has passed the requisite tests, FISA issues a special chassis plate certifying that it has been deemed raceworthy.

*When a chassis has passed the requisite tests, FISA issues a special chassis plate certifying that it has been deemed raceworthy.*

# CHAPTER 8

# Engine, gearbox and driveline

*Money can't buy many of the engines used in Formula 1, because their manufacturers supply them exclusively – usually free of charge – as part of a comprehensive marketing and R&D strategy.*

## Sourcing an engine

Unlike the other senior categories of motor racing around the world – such as the American IndyCar series, in which every car is either powered by a Chevrolet, a Buick, or a Ford XB – the Formula 1 arena revolves around exclusive engine deals. The 1992 season was a case in point. Honda supplied engines (V12s) to the McLaren team – and no- one else. Mugen, a division of Honda, supplied engines (V10s) to the Footwork team – and no-one else. Yamaha supplied engines (V12s) to Jordan – no-one else.

Renault supplied engines (V10s) to just two teams, Williams and Ligier. Lamborghini did likewise, supplying engines (V12s) to Larrousse and Minardi. Ilmor also supplied engines (V10s) to two teams: March and Tyrrell. So, too, did Judd, supplying engines (V10s) to Brabham and the Andrea Moda *equipe*. As ever, the Ferrari works team ran with its own engines (V12s), but a supply was also made available to BMS Scuderia Italia. Another two-team deal.

Just *one* engine type, the Ford-Cosworth XB, was used by more than two teams – three teams, to be precise. Cosworth-developed Ford engines (V8s) were supplied to Benetton, Lotus and Fondmetal. There was a pecking order between these three: Benetton was treated as the 'works' Ford team, and therefore received the latest-series engines, Lotus was next in line, and Fondmetal was another rung down.

Money can't buy many of the engines used in Formula 1, because their manufacturers supply them exclusively – usually free of charge – as part of a comprehensive marketing and R&D strategy. The

deals between Renault and Williams, Honda and McLaren, and Yamaha and Jordan have typified such arrangements in the recent past.

Sometimes, engines are made available on a 'preferential terms' basis. This type of arrangement existed between the Ferrari factory and BMS Scuderia Italia, the latter paying around $6.5 million (£4 million) for its supply of works-prepared V12 Ferrari engines in 1992. Several other teams may have been able to match this price, but were not given the opportunity to do so, simply because a special commercial relationship exists between Ferrari and BMS Scuderia Italia.

At the opposite end of the scale, the Ilmor, Judd and Lamborghini engines can be regarded as 'customer engines', in that if a team owner approaches any of these manufacturers with a sufficient financial inducement, he's likely to secure a supply of their products.

In the period prior to the partnership with BMS Scuderia Italia, sponsorship coordinator Brian Sims recounted Lola's difficulties on the engine front: "It became increasingly obvious that getting a competitive engine package was slipping further away from us. Engines were steadily being committed elsewhere, Honda was pulling out of Formula 1, and it was getting more difficult to find the right engine.

"That was very important to us, because we didn't want to go into Formula 1 for the sake of being there. We wanted to be competitive."

In the event, Lola's engine problems were resolved when the supply of Ferrari's V12 units became but one element of the collaborative arrangement with BMS Scuderia Italia.

## Engine installation

FISA regulations stipulate that Formula 1 engines must be normally aspirated, and limit their capacity to 3.5ltr. Turbocharging, having become virtually universal following Renault's introduction of the first of the new generation of 1.5ltr forced induction Formula 1 engines in 1977, is now outlawed.

The Lola BMS-Ferrari T93/30's engine was the M7 version of Ferrari's fuel-injected V12 unit, with gear timing and cylinder banks with a sixty-five-degree included angle. Like all modern Formula 1 engines, it was cantilevered out from the rear wall of the chassis as a fully-stressed structural member, carrying loads from the gearbox, rear suspension and rear aerofoil ensemble through the car. There were four attachment points with the chassis: two at the top and two at the bottom. The two at the top were spigot-type mountings, located on either side of the cylinder head, that attached to circular load spreaders at the top of the rear wall

of the chassis. The two at the bottom were located on either side of the base of the crankcase and bolted to two aluminium brackets that were bonded and bolted to the lower edge of the rear of the chassis.

It's common for Formula 1 teams to build a full-scale mockup of the chassis/engine combination prior to constructing the actual car. This enables designers to troubleshoot the inevitable problems: in particular, checking clearances. Verification of the proposed engine installation is one key use to which the full-scale mockup is put.

The full-scale mockup for the Lola BMS-Ferrari T93/30 was initially based on a surplus Formula 3000 Lola chassis – logical, since the chassis of the new Formula 1 car was to be based on that – with an enlarged fuel cell area delineated in plywood, a pair of mockup radiator assemblies, again built from plywood, and an actual Ferrari V12 engine. The engine was devoid of internals, but was outfitted with all

*Unlike the other senior categories of motor racing around the world – such as the American IndyCar series, in which every car is either powered by a Chevrolet, a Buick, or a Ford XB – the Formula 1 arena revolves around exclusive engine deals. This is the Yamaha V12 engine, supplied exclusively to Jordan in 1992, then switched to Tyrrell (pictured) in 1993.*

135

It's common for Formula 1 teams to build a full-scale mockup of the chassis/engine combination prior to constructing the actual car. This is the full-scale mockup of the Lola BMS- Ferrari T93/30, with the fuel cell area and radiators represented in plywood, and a genuine Ferrari V12 engine.

its ancillaries and pipework, a trumpet tray, an induction system, a fuel system, twin exhaust manifolds, and an AP clutch unit. A peep inside the inlet trumpets revealed that the engine had been filled with an epoxy foam at the Ferrari factory to keep the inlet manifold profiles and other internal details from prying eyes!

To provide an accurate dimensional guide, all of these elements were mounted on a large plywood platform that was marked with a grid denoting incremental 4in (100mm) units of measurement. Lines delineating the car's planform were also applied to the platform, so that those tasked with outfitting the mockup could rapidly identify where the outer boundary lay and always work within it. The mock-

up's wooden elements were retained to the base board with small aluminium brackets, the plywood screwed, glued, and tacked together.

At a later date, the Formula 3000 chassis was eased away from the wooden elements of the mockup and replaced with a truer representation of the Formula 1 chassis. This was a mockup chassis made from the actual molds that had by this time been produced for the Lola BMS-Ferrari T93/30, the only difference being that the mockup chassis was made from fiberglass, not carbon fiber. A pair of mockup radiator ducts, left and right, were built onto the upgraded chassis mockup: the actual ducts were to be made from carbon fiber. The flat surfaces were represented in plywood, while surfaces with pronounced curvatures were reproduced using pieces of corrugated plastic board and lengths of masking tape. In the interests of practicality, the radius along the top edges of the radiator inlet ducts wasn't represented. For the most part, however, the ducts were accurate to within 0.04in (1mm), in common with the rest of the mockup.

The grid of measuring lines was extended up from the plywood base to encompass the mockup radiator ducts, creating a three-dimensional matrix of reference points.

There was a reason for representing the external parameters of the radiator ducts, rather than the sidepods themselves. Various items of equipment, primarily electrical, had to be mounted in the narrow gaps between the outer walls of the radiator ducts and the inner walls of the sidepods, and it was necessary to ensure that there would be adequate clearances. Furthermore, there was to be an even narrower gap – just 0.6in (15mm) – above the top of the radiator duct, through which the wiring looms associated with this equipment had to pass (mostly into the engine compartment) with sufficient clearance to prevent chafing.

Most of the equipment that would be housed on the radiator ducts was associated with the engine management system. When it came to selecting an suitable system from the range produced by the Italian manufacturer Magneti Marelli, one of Lola BMS-Ferrari's technical sponsors, the design team eventually opted for the same one installed aboard BMS Scuderia Italia's Ferrari V12-engined Dallaras in 1992, thereby benefiting from the race technicians' familiarity with it.

All of the engine management system black boxes, with the exception of a few that were going to be

*Rear view of the full-scale mockup. The various elements were mounted on a large plywood platform that bore lines delineating the car's planform, so that those tasked with outfitting the mockup could rapidly identify where the outer boundary lay and always work within it.*

A view of the rear wall of the Lola BMS-Ferrari T93/30's chassis following application of a layer of heat resistant aluminiumized material. The tank hatch – situated on the sloping rear deck of the chassis – is a mockup made from plywood, with shaped pieces of Ureol representing the various fittings.

Like all modern Formula 1 engines, the Ferrari V12 was cantilevered out from the rear wall of the chassis as a fully-stressed structural member. There were four attachment points with the chassis: two at the top and two at the bottom. Pictured is one of the spigot-type upper mountings, complete with circular load spreaders.

mounted behind the rollover bar, were to be carried on the radiator ducts. Actual examples of the hardware in question – including the telemetry transmission and pickup boxes – were installed in the appropriate locations on the mockup. Temporary retention methods were employed pending definition of the final configuration: Velcro patches, tiewraps and the rubber mounts with integral threaded metal posts that are traditionally employed on race cars to electrically insulate items of electrical equipment from the rest of the car, and also to protect them from excessive vibration.

In the middle of January 1993, just two months before the season's inaugural Grand Prix, three Italian technicians – one from Magneti Marelli and two from the Technoelettra company, based in Reggio Emilia – visited the Lola factory to make a dummy wiring loom. They brought with them a loom from the previous season's Dallara and tailored it to suit the layout of the Lola BMS-Ferrari T93/30. Connections were made with aircraft-type multipin plugs.

Like all modern Formula 1 cars, the Lola BMS-Ferrari T93/30 carried telemetry equipment. As well as relaying data pertinent to engine performance – such as the throttle position, and the radiator and exhaust manifold temperatures – the system could telemeter other parameters, such as steering inputs and suspension movements. The telemetry transmitter was housed under the damper hatch.

At the rear of the radiator duct mockups were the mockups of the water and oil radiators themselves (for the record, the Ferrari V12 engine runs on oil specially developed by Agip). Preliminary wind-tunnel tests had indicated, some time before the full-scale mockup was assembled, that the radiator layout originally envisioned would not satisfy the cooling demands of the Ferrari V12. Therefore, it was radically altered. In Eric Broadley's original concept, the radiators were angled forwards to improve the car's overall weight distribution – putting more weight forward. This reflected the layout of the company's recent Formula 3000 designs and its earlier Formula 1 designs for the Larrousse team. However, the Ferrari V12 engine has particularly high heat rejection requirements, and became clear that either larger water radiators must be specified, or their orientation had to be significantly altered. The former course of action would have resulted in oversized sidepods, incurring a variety of aerodynamic penalties. Therefore, the radiators were angled back-

An Italian technician helps to tailor the wiring loom. Most of the engine management system black boxes were carried on the radiator ducts. Hardware was installed on the full-scale mockup first. Connections typically are made with aircraft-type multipin plugs.

Views of the outer and inner surfaces of the radiator ducts. Visible on the outer surface are the rubber mounts with integral threaded metal posts that are traditionally employed on race cars to electrically insulate items of electrical equipment from the rest of the car, and also to protect them from excessive vibration.

*A radiator duct viewed from the front, following fitment to the chassis.*

141

Mounting brackets for the engine management system black boxes installed on the left radiator duct.

A carbon fiber tray, sandwiched between the tank hatch and the engine air intake duct, carried the Engine Control Unit (ECU): the device that regulates the ignition system mapping.

wards to provide a better throughput of air – the compromise to weight distribution being deemed the lesser of two evils.

The sidepods were redesigned to accommodate the new radiator configuration and a revised 1/3-scale model was tested in the windtunnel, confirming that the cooling capability was greatly enhanced.

A variety of factors have conspired to make cooling a contemporary Formula 1 engine difficult. Radiator layouts are asymmetric, because the water radiator on one side has to be much smaller than its counterpart on the other side to make room for a single oil radiator. In the case of the Lola BMS-Ferrari T93/30, there was a single all-water radia-

tor on the left side of the car, and a twin-radiator ensemble on the opposite side, split vertically, in which a water radiator accounted for the inner third of the total surface area and an oil radiator accounted for the outer two-thirds.

The normal way to achieve a balanced water cooling capability in these circumstances is to install a figure-of-eight pipework layout. This makes maximum use of the *overall* cooling potential by distributing it evenly to both water radiators. In the case of the Lola BMS-Ferrari T93/30, this was not feasible, because the Ferrari V12 engine has a most unusual cooling system arrangement in which a single water pump operates via a split-flow system to inde-

*The left radiator duct, bedecked with engine management system black boxes.*

143

*Wiring loom of the Lola BMS-Ferrari T93/30. A loom from a Dallara 192 raced the previous season by BMS Scuderia Italia served as an initial guideline.*

pendently cool the left and right cylinder banks, mixing the water at the pump inlet valves. Other Formula 1 engines either have two pumps – one for each bank – or the water is mixed at the outlet valves and passed through either one or two radiators, then passed back through the pump. In both cases, the cooling effect is equalized.

When attempting to determine how large the water and oil radiators need to be, the designers hold discussions with technical representatives of radiator core manufacturers with a specific interest in Formula 1. Lola Cars' supplier is the French company Secan. The designers furnish predicted airflow figures and the radiator manufacturer assesses what the heat rejection capabilities are likely to be, based on previous experience, then recommends radiator sizes. A windtunnel model with radiators scaled to the recommended size is then tested, and the pressure differential between the front and rear faces is measured (it's necessary to establish a lower pressure behind the radiator in order to draw the air through in the correct direction). The designers compare the windtunnel figures with what they expected to see. If the figures correspond, they proceed with radiators of that size. If the figures turn out to be slightly better – showing an average pressure drop

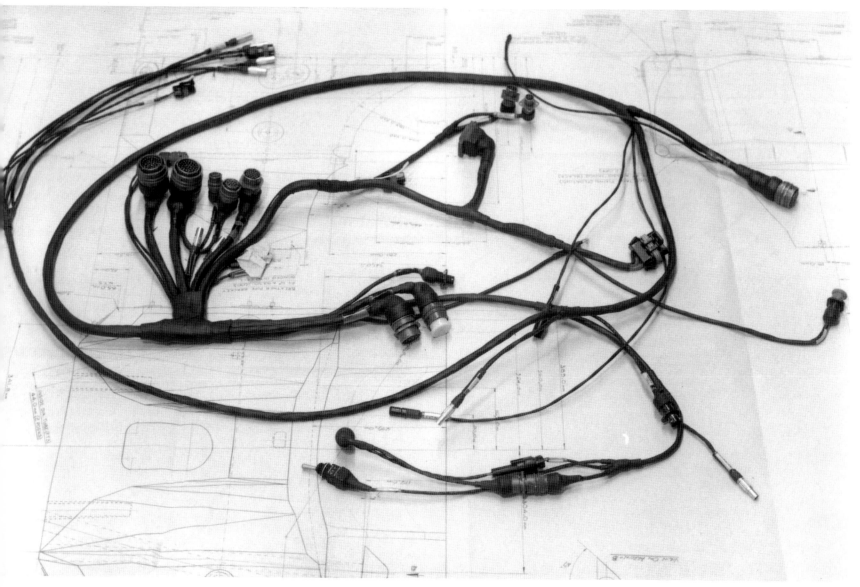

Formula 1 radiator layouts are asymmetric, because the water radiator on one side has to be much smaller than its counterpart on the other side to make room for a single oil radiator. This is the Lola BMS-Ferrari T93/30's right water radiator, which accounted for the inner third of the total radiator surface area on that side, the oil radiator accounting for the outer two-thirds.

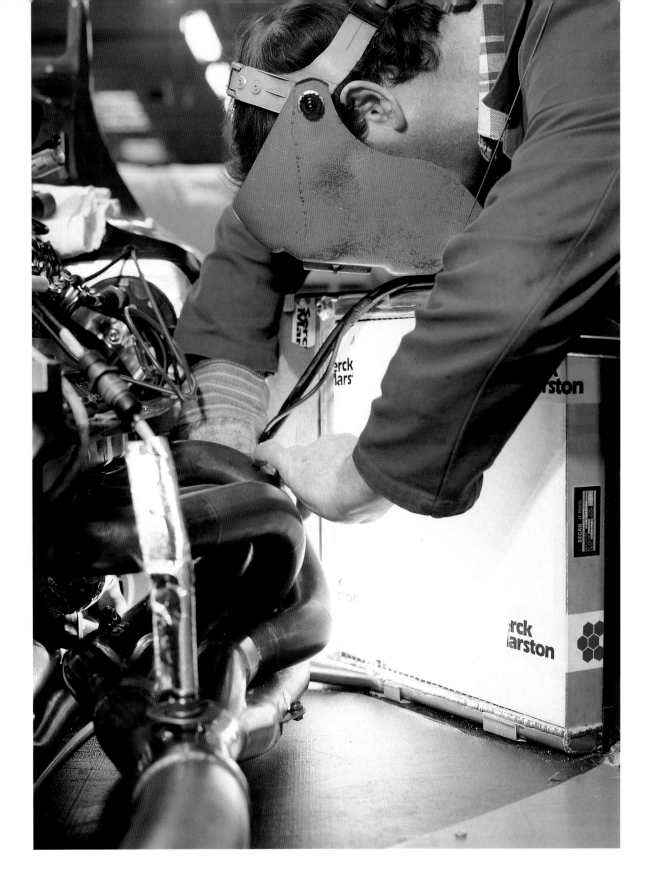

*A technician welds unions into the cooling system pipework.*

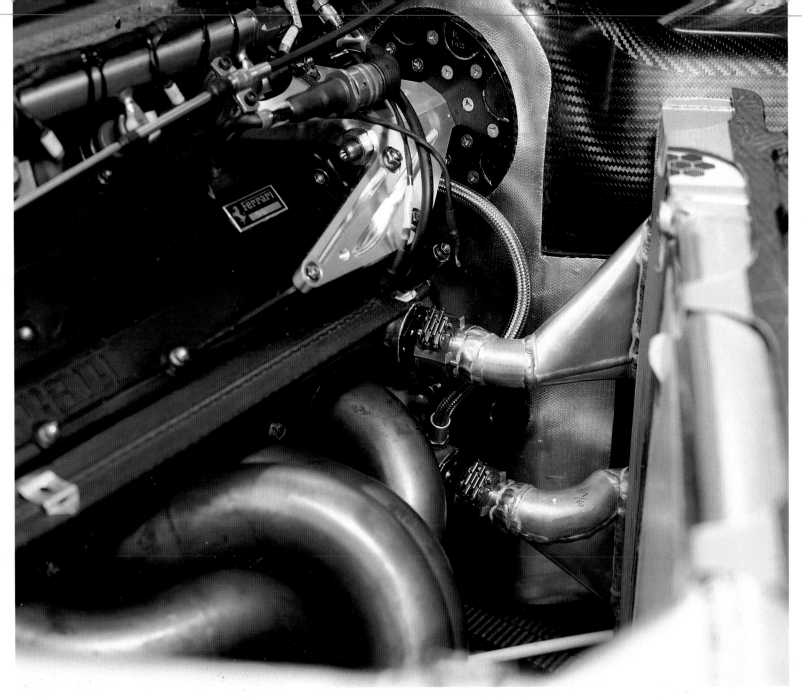

slightly higher than predicted – they can probably specify radiators with slightly smaller core face areas than originally anticipated, thus reducing aerodynamic drag. Conversely, if the figures prove to be slightly worse, they will have to either improve the quality of the airflow delivered to the radiators or specify slightly larger core areas and accept the drag penalty.

Designers must ensure that the radiator cores will always work within the pressure-differential parameters they're designed to accommodate, or they will be unable to function effectively. Their aim is to achieve the smallest core area possible by achieving the optimum efficiency – heat rejection capability – for a given core area. The radiator ducts are then sized to deliver the required volume of air. Windtunnel tests are aimed at achieving an even airflow distribution across the entire face of each radiator core, because if the duct shape is inefficient, a certain amount of the radiator won't be used and

*Close-up view of the right water radiator's unions with the Ferrari V12 engine. Wiggins fittings are employed, as opposed to hose clips, as they tend to be more reliable.*

147

*Split radiator arrangement (water and oil) on the right side of the Lola BMS-Ferrari T93/30. Designers aim to achieve the smallest core area possible by achieving the optimum efficiency – heat rejection capability – for a given core area.*

its full capability will not be exploited. The radiators would have to be larger to compensate.

It's usual for another specialist company to integrate the tank and connections with the radiator cores: in the case of the Lola BMS-Ferrari team, these tasks are undertaken by Serck Marston. Wiggins fittings, as opposed to hose clips, are employed to plumb the radiators into the car's pipework, as they tend to be more reliable.

The configuration of the cooling system is dic-

tated, to a certain extent, by the engine plumbing. In the case of the Lola BMS-Ferrari T93/30, the Ferrari factory supplied engineering drawings that indicated the connecting points for the oil and water systems. The car's designers then married these to the radiators in a manner conducive to their other requirements.

All Grand Prix cars feature Formula 1's equivalent of a water header tank. Instead of being mounted in an elevated position, however, this is mounted on

148

*Mesh is installed in the radiator ducts to protect the delicate radiator cores from foreign object damage.*

*The cylindrical blue object mounted on the right radiator duct is Formula 1's equivalent of a water header tank. Known as an air spring tank, it is normally occupied approximately one-third with water and two-thirds with air.*

the same level as the engine. Known as an air spring tank, the device is tapped into the (pressurized) cooling system. It is normally occupied approximately one-third with water and two-thirds with air, but as the water temperature rises – during a pit stop, for example, when the lack of cooling air is exacerbated by appreciable heat soak from the engine – the water level within the cylinder rises, compressing the air above it. As the water cools when the car returns to the racetrack, the water level drops

and the air pressure returns to ambient. Of course, a conventional 'total loss' system would perform the first function of this sequence perfectly well, pumping water out onto the pit lane while the car is at rest. The problem would only arise when the car went back out onto the racetrack and the water began to cool down again, because there'd be no water left to act as a cooling medium.

On the Lola BMS-Ferrari T93/30, the air spring tank was mounted on the right radiator duct. Lola Cars

*A cardboard mockup of the fuel cell was produced to facilitate fit checks in the chassis.*

manufactures its own air spring tanks.

FISA regulations stipulate that the entire fuel load must be carried in an approved safety cell: a flexible bladder that deforms in the event of a major impact, rather than rupturing with potentially disastrous consequences. The regulations state that no fuel can be housed ahead of the driver's back. The fuel capacity is specified by the engine manufacturer, taking in account every nuance of the engine's fuel consumption characteristics. It is the quantity of fuel required to cover the full Grand Prix distance – refuelling is not permitted in Formula 1 – with an adequate, though very small, reserve. The race-car designer's aim is to accommodate the cell in the smallest possible volumetric space within the chassis.

In the case of the Lola BMS-Ferrari T93/30, the fuel cell was initially schemed by Eric Broadley, then detailed design work was entrusted to a member of the design team: "The chassis was almost designed

*The Lola BMS-Ferrari T93/30's fuel cell, viewed from the front. Note the tunnel, half-way down the right side of the front face, through which the gear linkage passed.*

before the fuel cell came to me, so I had to get in there and ensure that we could get the volume required for the engine's needs."

The shape of the fuel cell should be such that the fuel pickup is constant, and that fuel cannot be trapped out of reach of the lift pumps. It is usual for Formula 1 cars to have three lift pumps: two that start operating as soon as the ignition is switched on, plus one reserve pump that the driver can activate towards the end of the race to ensure that

every last drop of fuel is scavenged. The third pump also serves as a backup, because if a pump starts to run dry as the fuel load gets low, it can fail. The three lift pumps deliver fuel to the collector, an acorn-shaped device that provides a constant supply to the mechanical pump that feeds the engine – and is, in turn, driven by it.

The fuel collector installed in the Lola BMS-Ferrari T93/30 was manufactured by Lola Composites from carbon fiber, and incorporated a system of baffles

to prevent surging. The fuel pump was a standard Ferrari unit, supplied with the engine, while the lift pumps were standard units produced by AC-Delco. Surprisingly, Formula 1 cars have street-specification automotive pumps, only slightly modified (in respect to their mountings).

To ensure that the lift pumps can scavenge all of the available fuel, and to limit the movement of fuel under inertial forces – because it would be detrimental to the car's handling – baffling is incorpo-

rated within the safety cell. Different designers specify different baffling configurations. The Lola BMS-Ferrari T93/30 had a single vertical baffle located across the entire width of the fuel cell floor.

The Lola BMS-Ferrari T93/30's fuel cell was manufactured to the designer's detailed specification by Premier Fuel Systems, a company based at the Donington Park racetrack. Its design only differed from the fuel cells specified by other Formula 1 teams in minor detail. A cardboard mockup was produced

*The same fuel cell, viewed from the back. Note the two tunnels through which the upper engine mount bracing tubes passed.*

153

Three lift pumps deliver fuel to the collector, an acorn-shaped device that provides a constant supply to the mechanical pump that feeds the engine – and is, in turn, driven by it.

The tank hatch, or tank top, is cast in magnesium and carries the fuel filler valve and the air vent valve, the fuel feed pipe/fuel return pipe 'break-away' valve combination (if the engine becomes detached in an accident, this prevents fuel flowing from the cell), and the drain pipe fitting.

154

*Installation of the tank hatch, which serves as the interface between the fuel cell and the sloping rear deck of the chassis.*

155

*Laying-up carbon fiber on the mold for the engine air inlet duct, or snorkel – the curving carbon fiber tunnel that carries air down from the streamlined aperture in the rollover hoop to the trumpet tray.*

beforehand for fit checks in the chassis.

Before the actual fuel cell was installed in the chassis, holes were drilled in the sides of the fuel cell compartment to accommodate bonded-in top hat fittings that would anchor the cell to the chassis walls to prevent it shifting under high cornering loads.

Various items of fuel system hardware were represented on the full-scale mockup to allow clearances to be checked before the race car itself was assembled. The interface between the fuel cell and

the sloping rear deck of the chassis – known as the tank hatch, or tank top – was mocked-up in plywood. The mockup hatch carried shaped pieces of Ureol representing the fuel filler valve and the air vent valve, together with the fuel feed pipe/fuel return pipe 'breakaway' valve combination (if the engine becomes detached in an accident, this prevents fuel flowing from the cell). There was also an actual drain pipe fitting (the device through which the remaining fuel can be drawn from the cell, allowing the fuel

The engine air inlet duct prior to installation. The design of the duct should ensure·that air is delivered to the engine as free of turbulence as possible to ensure that all of the cylinders receive an equal supply.

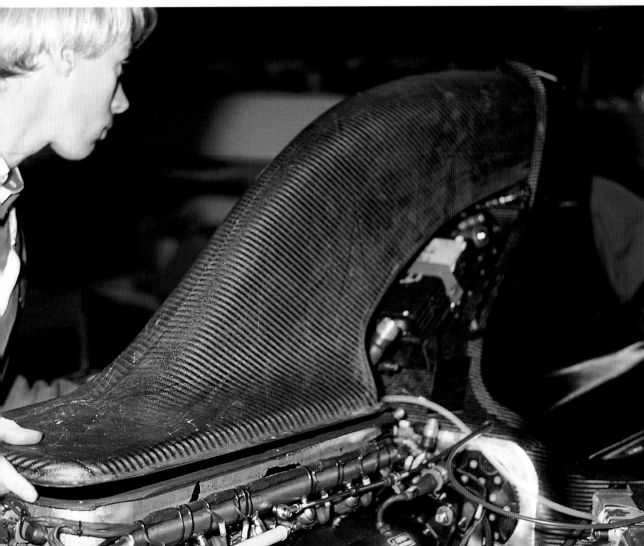

Installing the air inlet duct between the trumpet tray and the rollover hoop.

consumption to be precisely quantified – by subtracting the quantity drawn out from the quantity put in). The tank hatch itself was cast in magnesium. It was a redesigned version of Lola's existing Formula 3000- specification tank hatch, but employed identical fittings.

Mounted immediately above the tank hatch mock-up on an aluminium tray – representing the actual carbon fiber version – was a Magneti Marelli ECU (Engine Control Unit): the device that regulates the ignition system mapping.

Other important facets of accommodating a Formula 1 engine concern the efficient induction of air to sustain the combustion cycle and the expulsion of the resulting gases. Great care is required when determining the shape of the air inlet duct,

In the interests of optimizing the exhaust pipe tuning, the 'standard' system – as installed in the works Ferraris – was completely redesigned aft of the engine mounting plates. Installed in both pipes were tiny sensors (known as Lambda sensors) that continuously sample the oxygen content of the exhaust emissions.

159

*Close-up view of one of the Lola BMS-Ferrari T93/30's two Lambda sensors, which nestled in the outer ends of both exhaust manifolds. They relay data directly to the engine management system.*

or snorkel – the curving carbon fiber tunnel that carries air down from the streamlined aperture in the rollover hoop to the trumpet tray. Consideration must be given to the engine's air mass flow requirements, and the air must be delivered to the engine as free of turbulence as possible to ensure that all of the cylinders receive an equal supply. Following a series of dynamometer tests at Maranello, Ferrari

engineers defined an engine air inlet shape that fulfilled these requirements, and the designers of the Lola BMS-Ferrari T93/30 did their best to incorporate it into their preferred engine cover/rollover hoop shape.

At the opposite end of the combustion cycle, the exhaust system was designed and manufactured by Ferrari to conform to the Lola BMS-Ferrari team's

*A rare glimpse into the trumpet tray of the Ferrari Formula 1 engine, revealing the twelve inlet ports.*

requirements with respect to the points at which the pipes should protrude through the rear diffuser. In the interests of optimizing the exhaust pipe tuning, the 'standard' system – as installed in the works Ferraris – was completely redesigned aft of the engine mounting plates. Installed in both pipes were tiny sensors that continuously sample the oxygen content of the exhaust emissions. Known as Lambda sen-

sors, they relay data directly to the engine management system, which can adjust the air-to-fuel ratio to ensure that the engine is achieving complete combustion at all times.

The siting of many of the Ferrari V12 engine's ancillaries are dictated by the Ferrari works team to suit the specific requirements of the factory-run chassis, so the Lola BMS-Ferrari team had no option

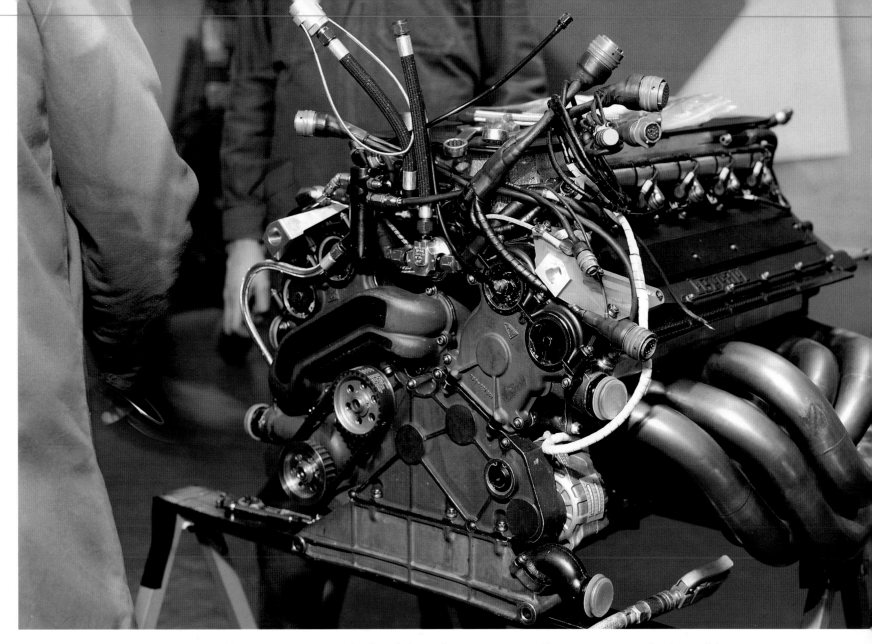

but to ensure that their chassis would be compatible with them. Various ancillaries were given fit checks on the fiberglass chassis mockup before being installed on the actual race cars. One, a crankcase pressure sensor mounted on the rear wall of the chassis on the right side, detects blow-past on the pistons to provide advance warning of a piston failure. Another, an alternator cooling duct, accepts a flow of bleed air diverted from the left sidepod and directs it into a shroud around the alternator. Made from carbon fiber covered with reflective tape to deflect heat from the engine, the duct was identical to that fitted to the Dallaras operated in 1992 by BMS Scuderia Italia.

The throttle butterflies were activated by a spring-loaded lever. A row of holes was drilled through virtually the entire length of the right side of the chassis to accommodate the throttle cable: through the sloping rear deck, through the seat back, through the driver's arm rest, and through the dash bulkhead to the accelerator pedal.

To determine the best route for the throttle cable and ascertain its length, this row of holes had been plotted earlier on the full-scale mockup. The task was undertaken by Lola Cars' Dave Scotney, who had responsibility for outfitting the mockup and went on to play a major role in assembling the actual race cars. A throttle linkage was mocked-up and

*The front of the Ferrari V12, revealing the engine's interfaces with the chassis, the ECU, and the fuel system.*

*The rear of the Ferrari V12, revealing the AP clutch unit and the engine's interfaces with the gearbox and the oil system.*

mounted on the engine block in the correct position relative to the throttle butterfly activator before the row of holes was drilled. At the initial entry point into the chassis, three holes – not one – were evidence of the fact that several attempts had been necessary to find the optimum spot. Scotney smiled: "That's the reason for building a mockup. We can make holes in a low-cost replica without making holes in the budget!"

The Lola BMS-Ferrari T93/30 was equipped with the first gearbox designed entirely by Lola Cars. A transverse gearbox, it was unusual by contemporary Formula 1 standards, in being designed with two distinctly different uses in mind: equipping the Formula 1 car and equipping Lola's production Formula 3000 cars for 1993 and beyond. For Formula 3000, a transverse gearbox was Lola's next logical step, because

it was a means by which the car's center-of-gravity could be moved forward. For that category alone, the financial investment in an all-new gearbox design could not be justified, but the prospect of a Formula 1 program made it a viable proposition.

The gearbox was designed with the facility to become semi-automatic at a later date, but the moratorium on 'advanced technology' proposed by FISA President Max Mosley late in 1992 and repeatedly espoused in certain circles thereafter, threatened to render this option obsolete.

In place of the Hewland FT range of ratios installed in the Formula 3000-specification gearbox, the Formula 1-specification version featured Hewland's high-technology, low-interia TPT ratios. The FT ratios employed in Formula 3000 are designed for long life, whereas the TPT ratios – being narrower and

lighter – need to be replaced more often, but this is perfectly acceptable in Formula 1, where budgets tend to be much higher. Low-inertia ratios are better, of course, because the engine doesn't have to accelerate such large lumps of metal. The Lola BMS-Ferrari team wasn't pioneering in this respect, for several Formula 1 teams used TPT ratios in 1992, among them Jordan, Fondmetal, Footwork – and, conveniently, BMS Scuderia Italia, so several sets of TPT ratios were carried directly over from the Dallara 192 to the Lola BMS-Ferrari T93/30.

XTRAC, a company formed by a former Hewland employee, supplies ratios to the majority of Formula 1 teams. McLaren, Williams, and several other teams, use David Brown ratios.

The oil employed to lubricate the gearbox – it's known as an EP (Extreme Pressure) oil – must be capable of withstanding exceptional levels of punishment, because the pressures between the gear teeth are phenomenal. Virtually the entire motive power of the engine is transmitted through a fingerprint-sized area of the gear tooth surface, and (theoretically, at least) metal never touches metal: contact is limited to the oil film. Consequently, the gear ratios seldom wear out.

In Formula 1, particularly, gearbox design is fraught with conflicting requirements, because limiting the weight of the gearbox is paramount. Most of the constituent elements represent weight that designers simply must accept, however. Steel is steel, after all, and there will always be a certain number of ratios and shafts within the gearbox, so a large percentage of the overall weight is unavoidable. It's essential to keep everything as compact as pos-

*Gearbox casing of the Lola BMS-Ferrari T93/30, with most of the internals installed. A transverse gearbox, it was designed with the facility to become semi-automatic at a later date, but moves to limit 'advanced technology' in Formula 1 looked likely to render this option obsolete.*

*The gearbox with rear suspension elements installed, but not the driveshafts.*

sible, because of the correlation between compactness and weight. As with all aspects of race-car design, though, there's a balance to be struck – because the designer must ensure that the gearbox is strong enough to provide structural support for the rear suspension pickup points, and rigid enough not to flex, because that would degrade the car's handling.

There is another reason for ensuring that the gearbox casing and the bulkheads within bestow sufficient rigidity. The gear ratios run to minute tolerances, and those must be maintained at all times to ensure that the moving parts don't deflect. Distortion attributable to heat must also be taken

into account.

The designer of the Lola BMS-Ferrari T93/30's gearbox: "Because this was our first 'box, the brief was to make it durable. We've succeeded in doing that with the 'box in Formula 3000 specification, but the minimum weight limit in that category is higher, so you can put more weight in to create the necessary rigidity. With the gearbox in Formula 1 specification, we've got to build down to a minimum weight limit that's forty kilograms less – with a bigger car – so weight is critical. Everything has to be stressed out. I made seventeen pages of notes just to stress one component. You don't want any extra metal in there."

One of the primary differences between the Formula 1 and Formula 3000 versions of Lola's new gearbox was the thickness of the casing, which was reduced in the Formula 1 version to save weight.

Aerodynamics are another influence on the design of the gearbox, because the rear diffuser must be kept as clear as possible of obtrusions. Windtunnel testing dictates what the undertray/diffuser profile is going to be, and if it's deemed that the diffuser angle should be very steep, it could have implications for the packaging of the gearbox. It would, of course, be possible to incorporate a bulge in the diffuser to accommodate the aft extremity of the gearbox, but that would impair its aerodynamic performance. The gearbox designer does his best to avoid such conflicts, but he has very limited scope to do so, because the overall layout of the car – with the cockpit, fuel cell, engine and gearbox arranged in series – 'pushes' the latter into the most prominent position.

When the Lola BMS-Ferrari T93/30 finally saw the light of day, about ninety-five percent of the gearbox was tucked away from the rear diffuser, creating only a minor bulge. As one might expect, transverse gearboxes are attractive from the packaging standpoint, because they minimize the extent to which the gearbox interferes with the shape of the rear diffuser.

*A complete driveshaft/upright/brake unit/axle assembly.*

167

# CHAPTER 9

# Aerodynamic aids

**During windtunnel testing, aerodynamicists 'tune' the length of the undertray, in concert with alterations they make to the diffuser shape, to achieve the optimum level of downforce.**

Of all the aerodynamic aids borne by Formula 1 cars, the most important is virtually invisible to the spectator: the undertray. FISA regulations stipulate that the undertray must be absolutely flat, with the exception of its outer edges, which may be curved upwards slightly – provided the radius of the curve does not exceed 2in (5cm). While designers can't incorporate any contoured features into the underside of the car to enhance its aerodynamic performance, they are free to introduce any amount of profiling into the diffuser – the upward-slanting aerodynamic device located immediately aft of the undertray – provided it doesn't protrude beyond the car's outer envelope, as viewed from above (planform).

The relationship between the undertray and the rear diffuser is key. Diffusers are shaped to create a localized low- pressure zone, because this helps to pull the rear of the car down onto the racetrack, increasing downforce – and, thus, traction. The diffuser draws on the air field beneath the undertray, so the low-pressure region actually extends forward into that zone, peaking at a point somewhere beneath the engine, and diminishing where it approaches the outer edges of the undertray.

During windtunnel testing, aerodynamicists 'tune' the length of the undertray, in concert with alterations they make to the diffuser shape, to achieve the optimum level of downforce. Note that their aim is achieve the optimum, as opposed to the maximum downforce: obtaining the maximum downforce isn't the sole objective, because designers are also concerned with the aerodynamic balance of the car, seeking to introduce stability by alleviating the unsettling effects of braking and acceleration. These actions

cause the car to pitch slightly, either nose-up (under acceleration), or nose-down (under braking), which in turn causes the center-of-pressure to shift forward or aft, destabilizing the car. The greater the extent of center-of-pressure shift, the more the car's stability is degraded. Therefore, designers attempt to minimize the center-of-pressure shift.

When aerodynamicists experiment with different diffuser shapes, they are not only concerned with optimizing downforce and reducing sensitivity to center-of-pressure shift for the reasons given above. They also try to utilize the flow of engine exhaust gases into the diffuser region, harnessing it to enhance the low pressure region at the rear of the car. Modern Formula 1 engines have a substantial throughput of air, and the effect of the exhaust gases entering the diffuser region is now so appreciable that, when the driver lifts his foot off the accelerator pedal, it has a pronounced influence on the aerodynamic efficiency of the car!

Two Ureol patterns are produced when manufacturing the undertray: one for the primary flat expanse, another for the rear diffuser element.

On the Lola BMS-Ferrari T93/30, four lengths of Bowden cable anchored the undertray to the top corners of the engine block, to ensure that its outer edges weren't pulled down by the low- pressure zone beneath the car. Other methods of restraint were employed elsewhere around its perimeter: for example, carbon fiber thongs connected the rear lip of the undertray to the rear aerofoil endplates. The Bowden cables were fitted to the full-scale mockup beforehand, to ensure that they would not foul the engine exhaust manifolds.

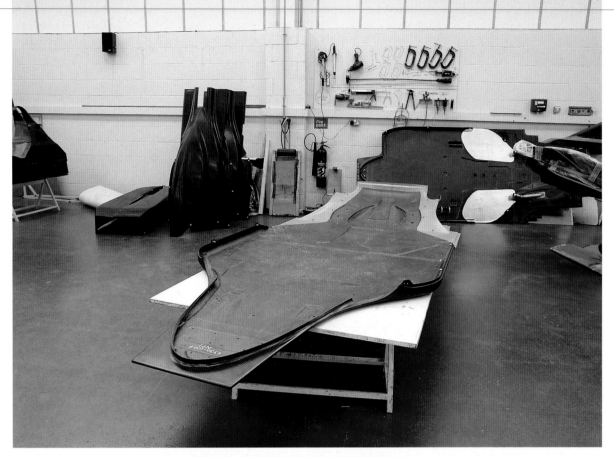

The undertray, acting in concert with the rear diffuser, creates a localized low-pressure zone that helps to pull the rear of the car down onto the racetrack, increasing downforce – and, thus, traction.

Fences and 'feet' on the lower surface of the rear diffuser channel the airflow to maximum effect.

169

The length of the undertray directly influences the length of the sidepods – the structures that house the radiator ducts and streamline the zones between the front and rear wheels – due to a FISA edict known as the 'shadowplate ruling.' This stipulates that the sidepods must not extend beyond the parameters defined by the undertray, as viewed from below – yet the length, height and shape of the sidepods have a bearing on the total lift-to-drag ratio of the car, which is another critical factor.

Senior designer Mark Williams: "The height of the sidepods is important, because it can influence the flow of air over the upper element of the rear aerofoil ensemble. There's a compromize to be made, because the sidepods must be tall enough to accommodate the radiators, but they mustn't be so tall as

*Various types of restraints anchor the undertray to the chassis and engine block, to ensure that its outer edges don't get pulled down by the low-pressure zone beneath the car. This restraint passes through the forward end of the right radiator duct.*

to interfere with the flow of air over the upper element of the rear aerofoil ensemble. Sidepod height also influences the flow of air over the car as a whole. The airflow, having passed over the front wheels, must transit the tops of the sidepods before passing over the rear wheels. The sidepod height has a bearing on the manner in which the airflow changes direction over those three regions, which in turn has

a bearing on the downforce generated by the body shape of the car, as distinct from the aerofoil ensembles.

"That includes the lower element of the rear aerofoil ensemble, which can effect the undertray, which in turn effects the total downforce. All of these parameters are interrelated."

The shape of the sidepod inlets is also impor-

*The carbon fiber/Kevlar engine cover. Note the elaborate contouring that accommodated the engine trumpet tray.*

*Fitting the left sidepod. The shape of the sidepod inlets must be such that a smooth flow of air is delivered to the radiators, otherwise the cooling system won't perform efficiently.*

tant. It's necessary to achieve the smoothest possible flow of air into the inlets, to ensure that the radiators will perform efficiently. In the case of the Lola BMS-Ferrari T93/30, the inlet shape was modified several times during the course of windtunnel testing. An array of pressure-tapping valves was mounted on a rake placed across one inlet face. By this method, Lola's aerodynamicists compiled a computer-generated map indicating the local air pressures across the full width of the inlet face.

*Close-up view of the two carbon fiber/aluminium honeycomb structures that support the rear aerofoil ensemble.*

*The four elements that constitute a rear aerofoil mainplane.*

A fully-assembled rear aerofoil mainplane.

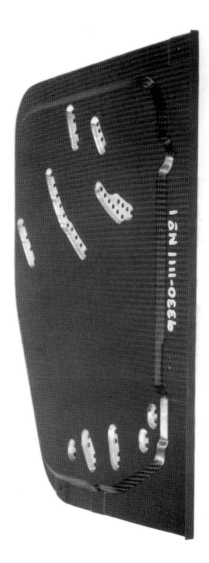

A rear aerofoil endplate. As can be seen, there is considerable scope for adjusting the angles of the aerofoil elements.

# CHAPTER

# 10

# The cockpit

Accommodating the driver in safety and comfort are vital design requirements. Formula 1 cars travel at very high speeds, so drivers must be well protected if they are to escape injury in the event of an accident. Grands Prix are run over considerable distances – races often approach two hours in duration – so drivers must be thoroughly comfortable if they are to perform to their full potential.

When a designer embarks on the task of scheming a new cockpit layout, he knows from past experience roughly where the key controls must be sited: the steering wheel, the gearshift lever, the bias adjuster for the braking system, and the foot pedals. Related tasks include incorporating the dashpanel, the driver's safety harness, and the fire extinguisher bottle: also – outside the immediate cockpit environment – the rear-view mirrors and, if the aerodynamicists have specified that the car should have one, a windshield.

In cases where the driver lineup is known in advance, the controls can be specifically positioned to suit them – or rather, to be more precise, the taller of the two drivers, because circumstances can result in either driver being assigned to a particular chassis. In the case of the Lola BMS-Ferrari T93/30, this was not possible: when the time came to finalize the cockpit layout, Michele Alboreto and Luca Badoer had yet to enter the picture. Therefore, the cockpit was schemed by the more usual method of placing a two-dimensional plastic representation of an 'average' driver on the drawing board. It has articulating joints that enable it to be appropriately positioned within the cockpit.

When Alboreto and Badoer were hired, the design-er responsible for scheming the cockpit obtained a set of measurements pertaining to their limbs and torsos. The specific measurements a designer must have to hand are: the overall length of the driver's torso, defined as the distance between his hips and his shoulders; the overall length of the driver's arms, and the distances between the joints – from the shoulders to the elbows, and from the elbows to the wrists; and the overall length of the driver's legs, and the distances between the joints – from the hips to the knees, and from the knees to the heels.

Using this information, the designer works outwards from what's termed the H-point – the point where the driver's hips will be situated within the cockpit. He must also make provision for: the driver's field of vision, so that he can survey the dashpanel through – and around – the steering wheel, have a direct line of sight to both rear-view mirrors, and view the racetrack ahead and to the sides; the articulation of the driver's legs and ankles, so that he can operate the foot pedals comfortably; and the articulation of his arms and hands, so that he can operate the steering wheel, the gearshift lever and the brake bias adjuster comfortably, and activate the ignition and other switches on the dashpanel.

All of this must be achieved in a manner that ensures compliance with a FISA safety regulation stipulating that the driver must be capable of exiting the cockpit within five seconds, without removing the steering wheel.

Of course, in configuring a cockpit to these parameters, a certain degree of adjustability must be designed into some of the controls – not just because either of the team's drivers may be assigned to a par-

The team's number-one driver, Michele Alboreto, sits in the cockpit of the Lola BMS-Ferrari T93/30 for the first time. The chassis was mounted atop two trestles in the prototype shop, devoid of all but a few fittings.

ticular chassis, but also because the drivers may wish to alter certain parameters to suit particular race-tracks. Therefore, the steering column must have the facility to be either raised or lowered, and the foot pedals must be adjustable fore and aft.

The cockpit layout of the Lola BMS-Ferrari T93/30 was verified using the same full-scale fiberglass/wood mockup that was used to define the engine instal-lation. The interior of the fiberglass chassis was outfitted with a plywood representation of the dash bulkhead, together with actual examples of the steer-ing column, the foot pedals, and some of the other controls.

Steering wheels for Formula 1 cars are supplied by specialist manufacturers such as Momo and Personal. Steering columns, on the other hand, are purpose built. The steering column for the Lola BMS-Ferrari T93/30 was machined from a solid bar of tita-nium for lightness, creating a precision tube some 30in (76cm) long. Formula 1 steering columns are manufactured in a similar manner to rifle barrels: they are drilled out in the same way to achieve the

*Steering wheels for Formula 1 cars are supplied by specialist manufacturers such as Momo and Personal. This is the Momo wheel fitted to Michele Alboreto's Lola BMS-Ferrari T93/30.*

requisite bore quality. At its lower extremity, the steering column was electron-beam welded to a titanium knuckle joint. The steering rack assembly comprized a cast magnesium housing with a titanium rack bar and other lightweight internals.

The Lola BMS-Ferrari T93/30 had a sequential gearshift system. Sequential systems allow the gearshift lever to be just that – a lever: it has fore and aft movement, and nothing else. There are several benefits to this type of system. Because the lever has no sideways movement across a gate, the driver can-

not accidentally select the wrong gear. Furthermore, there is no need for the designer to incorporate a 'blister' into the right side of the cockpit to accommodate the driver's hand, and there are none of the difficulties associated with creating adequate clearances between the gear lever and the steering wheel, and between the gear lever and the driver's right leg. The lever can be mounted very close to the steering wheel, minimizing the time taken to change gear.

When it came to determining the location of the

The steering rack assembly comprized a cast magnesium housing with a titanium rack bar and other lightweight internals.

gear lever in the Lola BMS-Ferrari T93/30, a lever was mocked-up in the cockpit of the fiberglass chassis mockup. Lola engineers climbed aboard the mockup to ascertain that the layout was a practical one, and that the downshift and upshift could be undertaken comfortably with a gloved hand. Pulling the lever backwards changed gear upwards, and pushing the lever forwards changed gear downwards. These informal tests fixed the position of the titanium pivot that held the gearshift lever. Lola Cars manufactures its gear levers in-house. They are machined from solid blocks of aluminium.

The gear linkage comprized six lengths of tubing: three of titanium and three of steel. To minimize frictional losses, a bellcrank was incorporated at the point where the linkage underwent its greatest angular diversion – where it passed through the seat back.

Formula 1 cars have a brake balance bar adjuster that is easily accessible to the driver, so he can alter the braking bias front to rear and vice versa while the car is in motion. The balance bar adjuster in the Lola BMS-Ferrari T93/30 was situated on the right side of the cockpit and was linked to the brake cylinders by a length of cable.

The Lola BMS-Ferrari T93/30's dashpanel was produced by Lola Composites from carbon fiber. One of the last components to be produced, it was designed to accommodate the Magneti Marelli cockpit instrumentation system. The switches were ergonomically sited with reference to the positions of the driver's hands and the location of the gearshift lever. Initially, a dashpanel was mocked-up from wood and aluminium – using a dashpanel from one of the Dallaras run by BMS Scuderia Italia the previous season as a pattern – and fitted to the full-scale fiberglass chassis mockup. The mockup dash was then shipped to Italy so that specialists from the Italian side of the partnership could outfit it, defining the new version.

Grand Prix cars are fitted with intercom systems

The Lola BMS-Ferrari T93/30 had a sequential gearshift system. Sequential systems allow the gearshift lever to be just that – a lever: it has fore and aft movement, and nothing else. Pulling the lever backwards changed gear upwards, and pushing the lever forwards changed gear downwards. Because the lever has no sideways movement across a gate, the driver cannot accidentally select the wrong gear.

*Front and rear views of the Lola BMS-Ferrari T93/30's dashpanel, which was produced by Lola Composites from carbon fiber. It was designed to accommodate the Magneti Marelli cockpit instrumentation system, with switches ergonomically sited with reference to the positions of the driver's hands and the location of the gearshift lever.*

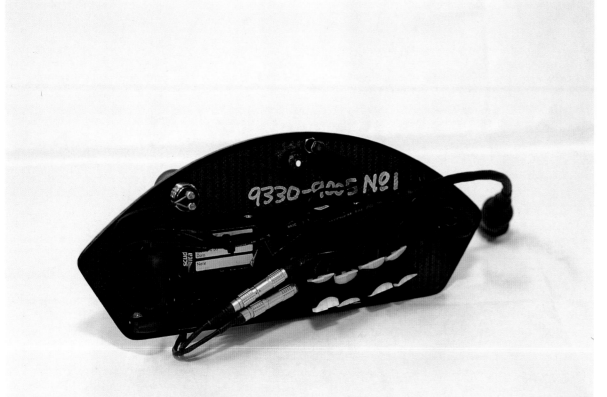

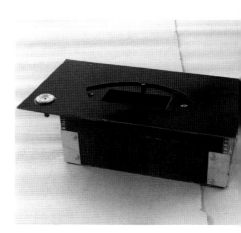

*This is the mold for the dashpanel, complete with 'eggboxing.'*

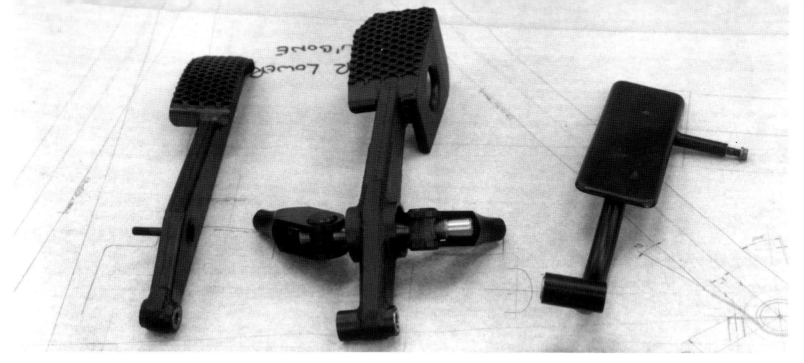

*The foot pedals prior to installation aboard the car.*

that allow the driver and his pit crew to exchange information verbally during races. On the Lola BMS-Ferrari T93/30, the radio unit was installed on the right radiator duct, and the transmit/receive antenna protruded from the top of the damper hatch. A small hole was drilled in the right side of the chassis to allow wiring from the driver's earphones and helmet-mounted microphone to pass from the cockpit to the radio unit.

Bolted into a recess on the cockpit floor was an anodized aluminium foot pedal mounting plate. The pedal arrangement in Formula 1 cars is identical to that of roadgoing cars. In the case of the Lola BMS-Ferrari T93/30, the accelerator pedal and brake pedal were the same as those fitted to Lola's production range of IndyCars and Formula 3000 cars, but the clutch pedal was specifically designed for Formula 1. All three pedals were manufactured in-house, from aluminium.

Also on the cockpit floor, in the space beneath the driver's knees, was a fire extinguisher bottle. Fitting an extinguisher to the full-scale mockup beforehand allowed the wiring routes for the fire suppression system to be checked before the installation was implemented on the race cars themselves. Fire extinguishers fitted to Formula 1 cars can be activated either from within the cockpit (by means of a push-button on the dashpanel), or from outside the car (by means of a pull-ring on the right side of the rollover hoop). They have two outlets: one to deliver extinguishant to a nozzle in the cockpit, and one to deliver extinguishant to a nozzle in the engine compartment. The nozzle in the cockpit was situated on the dashpanel, positioned so that it would direct extinguishant down onto the driver's legs, well away from his face.

Formula 1 cars are equipped with drivers' safety harnesses manufactured by specialist companies such as Willans and Sabelt. With the Lola BMS-Ferrari T93/30, the task of determining the correct locations for the safety harness anchors was undertaken with the full-scale mockup. The designer responsible for scheming the cockpit relayed the appropriate information to in-house composites engineer Roger Tyler, who incorporated inserts (local reinforcements) at the appropriate points in the carbon-composite/aluminium honeycomb structure, which was by that time at an advanced stage of design. The Lola BMS-Ferrari T93/30 had two inserts in the chassis floor to support the lap straps and crotch straps. Both fixings took the form of triple sandwich plates, through which the ends of the straps were woven. The shoulder straps were retained by dog's-bone fittings bolted into two inserts incorporated into recesses in the top of the seat back, and backed up by nut plates.

To provide an ergonomic environment for the driver within the chassis, and to create a clearance through which the gearshift linkage and various hydraulic and electrical lines could pass, two sculpted carbon fiber/Kevlar skins were bonded to the walls of the cockpit. They were contoured around the driver's sides to give him added support, and were recessed to accommodate his elbows and arm movements.

It's essential to ensure that the driver is comfortable in the car. The designer responsible for scheming the cockpit of the Lola BMS-Ferrari T93/30 elaborates: "You can engineer a car to the highest standards, but if the driver isn't comfortable he's never going give you his best, because he'll constantly be fighting to get comfortable. He'll feel that he's fighting the car, whereas he should feel at one with it.

"It's usually the first question, whenever a car is run. You concentrate on making sure that the driver is comfortable in the car. If he's not, you change whatever you have to change to make him comfortable, before you make any alterations to the car itself. If you don't, at a later stage in the proceedings he'll start saying, 'Something's hurting. I'm not comfortable,' and it's only then you realize that some of the information he's given you has been tarnished by his feelings of discomfort."

The first opportunity for one of the drivers to assess his new 'office' came in late-January 1993. Lola BMS-Ferrari's number-one driver, Michele Alboreto, flew in from Milan to join a small contingent from the Italian side of the partnership that was assisting Lola personnel to get the first car ready for its initial shakedown tests, at Portugal's Estoril circuit on 15 February. "I think it is important for the drivers to know how the car is made – the inside and all the parts – and follow the car as close as possible," he said.

Alboreto may have come to Huntingdon to gain familiarity with the overall construction of the car, but the dimensions of the cockpit were of particular interest to him. The chassis was mounted atop

*An unusual view of the foot pedals, and the hydraulic lines and cabling associated with the braking system. The pedal arrangement in Formula 1 cars is identical to that of roadgoing cars. The horseshoe-shaped feature visible from this angle is the rocker bulkhead.*

A view of the external fire extinguisher activation point: a pull-ring on the right side of the rollover hoop, distinguished by a mandatory E symbol. The fire extinguisher can also be activated from within the cockpit, by means of a push-button on the dashpanel. Note driver's head rest.

Formula 1 cars are equipped with drivers' safety harnesses manufactured by specialist companies such as Willans and Sabelt. This is the four-point Sabelt harness worn by the drivers of the Lola BMS-Ferrari T93/30. Fixings in the chassis floor took the form of triple sandwich plates, through which the ends of the straps were woven.

two trestles in the prototype shop, alongside the full-scale mockup, devoid of all but a few fittings. Alboreto clambered aboard and slid down into the contours of the seat back. He rapidly concluded that the cockpit was long and wide enough for both drivers to function well within it: "I will be comfortable in the cockpit, and this is very important to make aggressive races – because if you do not fit well in the car, maybe you can make the quick lap, but it's difficult to run properly for the race distance."

Although there was no steering column installed in the car at that stage, Alboreto had brought a steering wheel with him from Italy: a Momo wheel identical to the one he'd used the previous season at the Footwork team. "This is the size and shape I would like to use, but it's just to check if it's possible."

Alboreto took care to check that there would be no interference with his elbows or hands as he turned the wheel, then announced, "It will be perfect for me."

In addition to the 'Footwork' version, a different type of Momo steering wheel, with a narrower rim, had been brought to the Lola factory for fit checks. This had been removed from one of the Dallaras run by BMS Scuderia Italia the previous year. A pair of shoulder straps were removed from a safety harness, offered up to the appropriate positions on the seat back, and draped over Alboreto's shoulders. Although the dashpanel had yet to be fitted, Alboreto assessed his view of the instrument positions, and manipulated an imaginary gearshift lever, "...just to see where it will be in comparison with the steering wheel."

It was not possible, at that stage, to accurately assess the foot pedal positions, because the pedals had yet to be installed. Nevertheless, Alboreto felt that, given the scope for adjustment, there would be no discomfort involved in reaching them, and ample room to operate them.

Alboreto made particular mention of the build quality, praising the workmanship of the Lola personnel. He also stressed the importance of establishing good communications with those responsible for building the car: "I'm just staying close to the team, and talking – because the more we talk, the more things we can discover."

The vastly experienced Italian stayed at the factory until late that night, then flew back to Milan the following morning. He would return some weeks later, with team mate Luca Badoer, for the all-important seat fitting. This ensures that the driver is fully supported in the car against cornering, accelera-

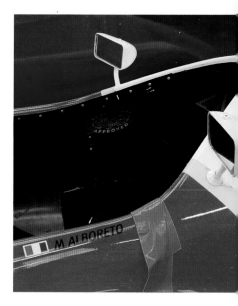

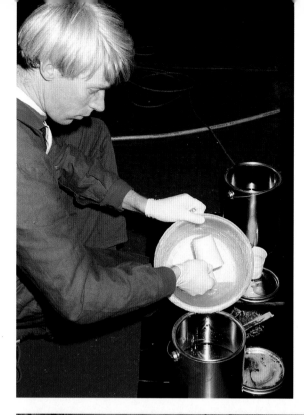

*Producing an equal mix of two agents that, shortly after contact, create a foam that will expand before solidifying, conforming exactly to the contours of the driver's body.*

*Technicians pouring in the mixture during Luca Badoer's seat fitting. While the chemical reaction takes place, the driver must maintain what he feels is a comfortable position in the car. He supports himself until the foam begins to harden, then – at the critical point when he feels the foam solidifying – he uses the bag as a seat, allowing it to support him.*

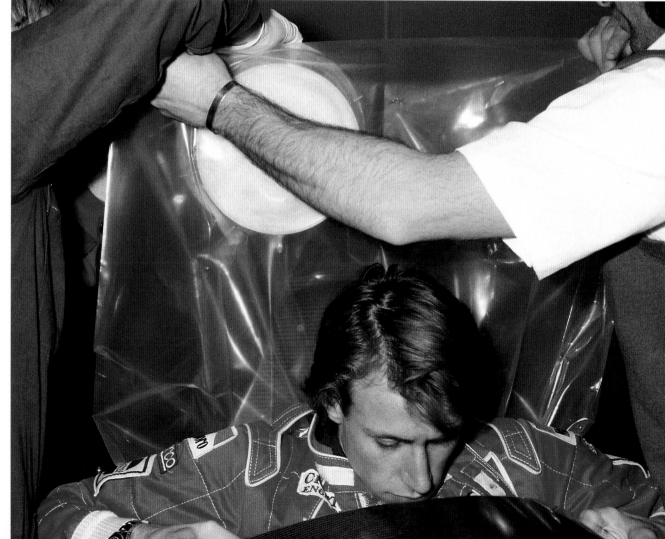

tion and deceleration forces, by creating the ultimate in tailored seats: a form-fitting seat profiled to his own unique shape. The first step is for a large plastic bag to be placed in the cockpit. The driver gets into the car and sits on the bag, the top of which is held open to allow an equal mix of two agents to be poured in. Shortly after contact, these create a foam that expands within the bag before solidifying, conforming exactly to the contours of the driver's body.

While this chemical reaction is taking place, the driver must maintain what he feels is a comfortable position in the car. He supports himself until the foam begins to harden, then – at the critical point when he feels the foam solidifying – he uses the bag as a seat, allowing it to support him. The resulting seat usually comprizes two elements: a back section and a bottom section – although it depends how tall the driver is and the way in which he sits in the car. Several coats of resin are applied to the foam afterwards. This hardens it further, ensuring that it will withstand the rigors of racetrack use.

Michele Alboreto surveys the fruits of his seat fitting. It can be seen that the seat usually comprizes two elements: a back section and a bottom section – although it depends how tall the driver is and the way in which he sits in the car.

Several coats of resin are applied to the foam to harden it further, ensuring that it will withstand the rigors of racetrack use.

# CHAPTER

# 11

# on the racetrack

**On March 14, 1993, the car made its debut at a Grand Prix meeting. The event was the South African Grand Prix, held at the Kyalami circuit outside Johannesburg.**

As soon as the first Lola BMS-Ferrari T93/30 was completed – in the wee small hours of a February morning – it was placed on a set of cornerweights and found to weigh just under 1,103lb (500kg) in its unpainted state: a confirmation of design calculations, but a relief to all concerned nonetheless. FISA's minimum weight limit of 1,114lb (505kg) includes 11lb (5kg) for the on-board TV camera equipment, if that is carried, or compensatory ballast if it is not.

Unusually, the engine couldn't be started, because Ferrari management stipulates that the company's technicians must be in attendance every time a Ferrari Formula 1 engine is brought to life, and that wasn't possible in the circumstances. Senior designer Mark Williams: "It's probably the first time a car's ever left here without having the engine fired-up. We normally fire the engine up to check whether there's any leaks, check everything turns over – just to check it's working, basically."

The car was soon loaded aboard the team's transporter, which then began the long journey south to the Estoril racetrack in Portugal, where Ferrari technicians waited alongside race team personnel to conduct initial shakedown tests. As is customary on such occasions, there followed a series of frustrating technical setbacks. When the engine was fired-up for the first time, the failure of an input bevel bearing in the gearbox silenced it before the car had left its axle stands. The failure was traced to an incorrect clearance.

With a replacement bearing housing fitted, the car was able to take to the racetrack for the first time. After about twenty laps, however, the gearbox suf-

fered a catastrophic failure. It transpired that debris resulting from the initial failure had found its way into one of the two gearbox oil pumps and sheared the drive. Without realizing it, the team had been running a car that wasn't flowing oil in left-hand corners, and had therefore been intermittently running dry. This, in turn, destroyed all the bearings.

Fortunately, a spare gearbox had been taken to Portugal. As a precautionary measure, this was fitted with oil pumps possessing a greater flow capacity. The car was run for the balance of the time available in this new specification, but there was insufficient time left to appraise it properly. The initial assessment by drivers Michele Alboreto and Luca Badoer was that the Lola BMS-Ferrari T93/30 was better balanced than the Dallara 192 that BMS Scuderia Italia had raced the previous season.

Shortly afterwards, the car was run again – this time at Italy's Imola circuit. It was too cold to be representative of Grand Prix conditions, and there was only a day and a half in which to run, but the team did make some progress.

On March 14, 1993, the car made its debut at a Grand Prix meeting. The event was the South African Grand Prix, held at the Kyalami circuit outside Johannesburg. Luca Badoer's car had minor gear-selection maladies. His was a brand new car that hadn't turned a wheel, so this was perhaps to be expected. Michele Alboreto's car featured a new suspension arrangement, front and rear: an attempt to improve grip. Although untested, the geometry resulted from experience gained in the limited running time at Estoril and Imola. However, time was tight once again. The rulemakers had deemed that there

Michele Alboreto pilots the unpainted car during shakedown tests at the Estoril circuit in Portugal. The cryptic legend on the engine cover – Wait for a new flavor – is a reference to the fact that primary sponsor Philip Morris was set to promote its Chesterfield brand, as opposed to Marlboro.

Alboreto in action during the Lola BMS-Ferrari T93/30's debut race, the 1993 South African Grand Prix at Kyalami.

*Alboreto negotiates a corner during the 1993 South African Grand Prix, with Alessandro Zanardi's Lotus in close attendance.*

would be a mere forty minutes of pre-race running time for the inaugural Grand Prix of 1993.

It was quickly discovered that the suspension set-up was wrong, so the team expended all of the available time on the first (Friday) practice session trying to do something about it. Overnight, Eric

Broadley devised a further geometry revision, which was run on the second and final practice session on Saturday. It worked very well, providing the team with a positive direction in which to go for the next Grand Prix, in Brazil. The loss of precious testing time at Estoril had yet to be redressed, however.

*Heading for new horizons: after months of intensive preparation, the car's maiden race outing.*

# Index